GOOGLE CLASS

A Comprehensive Guide for Teachers and Students to Learn about Detailed Features of Google Classroom to Conduct Online Classes Successfully and Managing Classes Effectively

By

Ali Keler

© **Copyright 2020 Ali Keler- All rights reserved.**

This document is geared towards providing exact and reliable information in regards to the topic and issue covered. The publication is sold with the idea that the publisher is not required to render accounting, officially permitted, or otherwise, qualified services. If advice is necessary, legal or professional, a practiced individual in the profession should be ordered.

- From a Declaration of Principles which was accepted and approved equally by a Committee of the American Bar Association and a Committee of Publishers and Associations.

In no way is it legal to reproduce, duplicate, or transmit any part of this document in either electronic means or printed format. Recording of this publication is strictly prohibited and any storage of this document is not allowed unless with written permission from the publisher. All rights reserved.

The information provided herein is stated to be truthful and consistent, in that any liability, in terms of inattention or otherwise, by any usage or abuse of any policies, processes, or directions contained within is the solitary and utter responsibility of the recipient reader. Under no circumstances will any legal responsibility or blame be held against the publisher for any reparation, damages, or monetary loss due to the information herein, either directly or indirectly.

Respective authors own all copyrights not held by the publisher.

The information herein is offered for informational purposes solely and is universal as so. The presentation of the information is without a contract or any type of guarantee assurance.

The trademarks that are used are without any consent, and the publication of the trademark is without permission or backing by the trademark owner.

All trademarks and brands within this book are for clarifying purposes only and are owned by the owners themselves, not affiliated with this document.

Table of Contents

Book 1: Google Classroom 2020

A Comprehensive Guide for Teachers and Students to Learn about Digital Google Classroom Management, and the Improved Quality Engagement during the Lessons

INTRODUCTION 9

CHAPTER 1: UNDERSTANDING GOOGLE CLASSROOM 12

1.1 What Is Google Classroom? 12

1.2 How Does Google Classroom Work? 16

1.3 Users of Google Classroom 19

1.4 Google Classroom for Elementary Grades 34

CHAPTER 2: BENEFITS AND FEATURES OF GOOGLE CLASSROOM 37

2.1 Advantages of Google Classroom 37

2.2 Google Classroom Features and Educational App 51

2.3 Hurdles While Using Google Classroom 67

2.4 What's New In Google Classroom? 72

CHAPTER 3: STARTING WITH GOOGLE CLASSROOM 76

3.1 Link Google Classroom 76

3.2 Explore Your Way through the Google Classroom 76

3.3 Start Your First Google Class 79

CHAPTER 4 MANAGING YOUR GOOGLE CLASSROOM... 84

4.1 Effectively Create Your Classroom Content....... 84

4.2 Adding an Assignment and grading it 97

4.3 Sharing Resources and Links 102

4.4 Keep Google Feeds Clean 104

4.5 Student Performance Management Tips 105

4.6 Encourage Collaboration between Students 110

CHAPTER 5: BASICS OF GOOGLE CLASSROOM FOR STUDENTS..113

5.1 Students' Managing Classes 113

5.2 Managing Assignments 118

CHAPTER 6: ADDITIONAL TIPS FOR USING GOOGLE CLASSROOM.. 127

CONCLUSION 139

REFERENCE 142

Book 2: Google Classroom 2020

An Easy Guide on How to Teach Digitally in 2020 and To Manage Your Google Classroom Effectively

INTRODUCTION **146**

CHAPTER 1: INTRODUCTION TO ONLINE CLASSROOMS **149**

1.1 What is Online Learning? 151

1.2 History of Online Education 154

1.3 Different Types of Online Classrooms 158

1.4 Various myths about online learning 162

CHAPTER 2: ADVANTAGES AND DRAWBACKS OF ONLINE LEARNING **167**

2.1 Advantages of Remote Learning 167

2.2 Limitations of Online Classrooms 174

CHAPTER 3: GETTING STARTED WITH GOOGLE CLASSROOM **181**

3.1 Introduction to Google Classroom 181

3.2 Features of Google Classroom 189

3.3 Simple steps for setting up Google Classrooms 220

3.4 Adding and Grading Assignments 223

3.5 Privacy Evaluation for Google Classroom 229

3.6 Apps for creating content for Google Classroom 233

CHAPTER 4: GOOGLE CLASSROOM-AN INTERACTIVE PLATFORM 238

4.1 Engagement through student-teacher interaction 238

4.2 Engagement through student-student interaction 242

4.3 Parental inclusion in Google Classroom 243

CHAPTER 5: GOOGLE CLASSROOMS-ADVANTAGES AND LIMITATIONS 245

5.1 Advantages of Google Classroom 245

5.2 Limitations of Google Classroom 250

CHAPTER 6: HOW TO GET THE MOST OUT OF GOOGLE CLASSROOM LEARNING? 252

CONCLUSION 259

REFERENCES 261

Google Classroom 2020

A Comprehensive Guide for Teachers and Students to Learn about Digital Google Classroom Management, and the Improved Quality Engagement during the Lessons

Introduction

Google Classroom is an online service designed to create educational tools, to teach online in a paperless way. This is achieved in such a way that teachers can give students assignments and review their performance, as well as make numerous informative announcements. The classroom offers fast integration with other services, including Gmail, Disk, and Dock, which are all part of the free Google Apps for Education services bundle.

The Google classroom was developed as a tool for educational purposes, as well as integrated with already popular tools like Gmail, Docs, and Drive. So, although there are currently several ways to automate classroom work on Google Drive. Google Classroom is ready to provide students with a universal workplace solution through quick integration with Google Drive, a user-friendly interface, and new opportunities that teachers need so much.

If you're a teacher and a student, you can take advantage of its unique features. Teachers can now communicate with students and even parents remotely and efficiently: setting tasks, reviewing student results, organizing notes and workflow, making announcements, and much more. You have all your teaching materials, lesson notes, and valuables in one place with Google Classroom, so you don't have much stress on organizing your Online Classroom. It's essential to understand the value of google classroom, which is a free web service that allows teachers to track student progress, distribute that delegate grading in a paperless way.

Teaching without using the online tools and resources will make the life of a teacher very difficult. The cycle of arranging student research takes up such a big part of the classroom time, ensuring that all are aware of the upcoming assignments and solutions. Teachers entering the world of classroom technology are not uncommonly frustrated by the additional computers, electronic documents, software, and classroom management techniques that students need to learn successfully. Several teachers have started using Google Classroom to help with Classroom Management, a platform developed with teacher input from the ground up.

Thanks to its step-by-step overview of this helpful software, Google Classroom helps you to spend more time teaching and less time on other things. One of the best online tools you can use to take your class to the next level is Google Classroom. This website enables you to connect, send emails, work on assignments and forums, and much more. As a teacher, with Google Classroom support, you'll appreciate all the stuff you can do.

It's easy to use and free, and with it, you can do a lot of things. Teaching can be a sort of a process, and getting it squared is sometimes tricky. Nevertheless, you can do that and much more with Google Classroom, so you can easily create engagement, attract students, so hold it. This also helps to communicate with friends, including seminars, behavioral problems, and even general announcements and notes.

This book is arranged as a practical guide that takes you through the process of understanding and gaining a more in-depth knowledge of google classrooms to reorganize operations of file sharing between students and their teachers. You will start by understanding what the google classrooms are all about, their fundamentals, who created it and its release date, the applications and features of google classrooms, and how to quiz. And in the final chapters, you can go through task correction strategies using google classrooms as well as their tips and tricks.

This book is packed full of knowledge to improve your understanding of google classrooms in action. It provides more practice opportunities and knows how to use it. If you want to learn more than how to use Google Classroom to effectively teach your students and make your classroom interactive, continue reading

Chapter 1: Understanding Google Classroom

Today's technology empowers educators to step away from the conventional classroom where teachers guide and students work independently; everyone does the same. You may have heard of it if you're a teacher, student, or even a parent. Most likely, several schools would turn to use this despite the current global situation. Maybe your school is beginning to turn to that form of program. If that is the case, you will probably know Google Classroom a little bit more. Here we'll help you to understand Google's classroom properly and how it works.

1.1 What Is Google Classroom?

Google Classroom is a classroom software platform designed to provide a single Dashboard to unify the use of other Google apps by teachers. Google Classroom aims to encourage paperless communication between teachers and students and streamline the workflow of education. Classroom lets teachers create classes, post assignments, organize files, and show real-time work.

Students can start their research with just one button, then view the assignment and then open a Google Doc. Teachers have a real-time perspective of student progress as they do so, and can provide suggestions along the way. Students have their own Google Drive folder that enables students and teachers to have permanent access to previous research, and inside the Classroom, educators can also allocate grades.

One of the good features is that the Classroom is completely compatible with all other Google apps, and students and teachers can easily exchange information with each other, instead of having to jump through multiple barriers to send work. It also simplifies other features in apps: for example, using the evil "Doctopus" feature to make Google Docs will no longer need duplicate copies for students.

In short, Google Classroom provides a one-stop platform to promote digital development, workflow, and teacher-student communication. Like other Google applications, it's available to schools for free, has no commercials, and also uses content from students or teachers for ads.

Google Classroom is a free resource for teachers and students to work with together. Teachers will create an online classroom, invite students to the class, then create assignments, and distribute them. Students and teachers can have discussions about the assignments inside the Google Classroom, and teachers can monitor the progress of the students. Schools must register to use the Classroom for a free account on Google Apps for Education.

Students and teachers have access to apps that aren't included in a personal Google account under Classroom software. For example, teachers can add images to questions in Forms, or as answers to multiple choices. Gmail's Inbox has grouped Classroom messages in Inbox, making it easier for teachers and students to find relevant notifications and highlights. The Classroom tool also helps teachers to organize the stream of classes by adding topics to posts, and teachers and students can search the stream for different subjects.

Google Learning helps teachers to create an online classroom environment where they will be able to access all the information their students need. Files are saved on Google Drive and can be edited in applications like Google Docs, Sheets, etc. But what distinguishes Google Classroom from the standard Google Drive experience is the interface between teacher and student, developed by Google for the way teachers and students think and work. The classroom is designed to help teachers build and collect paperless assignments with time-saving features such as the ability for each student to make a copy of a Google document automatically. This also generates Drive files for each task, which helps to keep everything coordinated for each project. Students will keep track of what's due on the Assignments page and start working just one click away. Teachers will easily see who completed the work or who didn't and provide clear, real-time feedback and grades right in the Classroom.

If you still use paper to a large degree for materials and assignments, then Google Classroom provides an easy-to-use, entry-level step towards digitalizing your class. As with many of its products, Google makes every effort to have a user-friendly and self-intuitive experience. If you still use paperless approaches for your pupils, then with its peerless integration with its devices, the Classroom can streamline your workflow.

This not only helps with coordinating students by placing all tasks and research in one safe place, but it also supports teachers. Creating, copying, assigning, supervising, processing, marking, recording, and returning students to work is a process that involves a lot of time and measures. Through merging, removing, or grouping these tasks, Google Classroom simplifies certain tasks. Google Classroom would certainly save teachers time and hassle grading student work.

The classroom is not a development tool, but rather a management tool; thus, it involves you and your students to know how to post information and records, and how to find the information you want. If your students already have experience with other Google apps, such as Docs or Spreadsheets, then Classroom is already set to use them.

Also, Google Classroom is designed to exchange ideas and tools with teachers and students. Teachers and students can engage in online Classroom discussions, and in forums or other communication platforms, everyone can post links to useful tools.

Google is entering an increasingly dynamic market filled with successful learning management systems for the Classroom. Its smooth integration with its software is where it has the most leverage. This allows students and teachers to have incredibly easy access to each other's work and eliminates many of the steps previously required to exchange knowledge. While other systems such as Schoology or Edmodo incorporate Google apps effectively into their systems, extra steps are needed, which means extra clicks and extra complications.

Another benefit is that products made with Google Apps are optimized for sharing, and sharing can be simpler at Google Classroom than other more "Closed Network" information management systems.

Google Classroom may lack some of the benefits teachers have come to enjoy with other systems like Schoolboy, which, over the past few years, has steadily extended its functionality. Some programs allow teachers to make assessments right in the application itself or more conveniently allow non-Google communication and resource resources to be used. Google describes Google School as "The school mission control," and that could be the best way to think about it. Simply put, it's a forum for teachers and students to connect Google's G Suite resources. It also serves as a digital repository where teachers can hold and exchange class materials with students — all of them paperless. From there, you can select which features you wish to implement. This simplicity, and its seamless integration with the popular Google apps, is possibly what has made Google Classroom one of today's most commonly used EdTech apps.

Does Google Classroom become an LMS?

In basic words, no. Google Classroom is not a stand-alone program for learning management (LMS), course management (CMS), or student information (SIS) program. That said, Google adds new functions to Google Classroom periodically. For example, in June 2019, Google announced that schools would soon be in a position to synchronize the new grading features of the tool with an existing student information system. When Google continues to add functionality, it is likely to start looking, becoming more like an LMS, to work. But it's better, for now, to think of the device as a one-stop-shop for class organizing.

1.2 How Does Google Classroom Work?

Anybody! Google Classroom is offered as a free platform for those with a Google personal account, and it is also free for organizations that use G Suite for Education or G Suite for Non-profits. In most cases, teachers and students can use a Google account offered by their school to access Google Classroom. Although the primary users of Google Classroom are teachers and students in classrooms, there are also features that administrators, families, and homeschoolers can use.

The classroom works with Google Docs, Google Drive, and Gmail to allow teachers to allocate students to work. The teachers will add to their assignments, papers, links, and photos. Both operations are performed remotely using a computer or mobile device.

Teachers should set the time when students see their assignments and attachments.

Students sign in to the Classroom, see and complete their upcoming research online. The teacher sees this on the Stream page when a student hands in work.

The instructor will post and set a due date for one or more classes or individual students in a class. When delegated, teachers manage access to any files they add.

When adding a Drive file (document, slides, or sheets), the instructor may choose to:

- Allow students to access the folder — all students may read the file, but not edit it.
- Allow file editing for students — all students share the same file and can edit it.
- Make a copy of each student's file — Students are given an individual copy of the file they can edit.

The name of the student is immediately appended to the title of the text. When a student hands in the assignment, the instructor shows the file labeled with the name of the student.

The instructor will monitor their progress as students work on an assignment, add notes, and make edits in the documents. Students may work on the assignment by viewing a document, editing a shared document, or editing a copy of a document by themselves. The students can add to their work files, links, or photographs. They hand in their job once done.

A student can submit research, make changes, and re-send it before the due date. Only the instructor has access to editing after the student turns in a file from Google Docs, Papers, or Slides and can make some modifications.

Unless you are using originality forms, Google will not store the content you apply for the report and will not claim ownership of the material. The material belongs to the students. We must keep your data safe. We are searching for what's freely accessible on the web, and we don't store originality records permanently.

How to Create a Class

Google Classroom helps teachers to create an online learning environment where they will be able to access all the information their students need. Teachers can make assignments from inside the class that their students complete and turn in for gradation.

The classroom comes with three key tabs. Here's what those tabs mean:

- **Stream:**

This is where you're handling your class assignments and creating class announcements. You may add new assignments with due dates and materials attached. On the left are the future tasks. You can even give a letter to your whole class – also with an attachment – and through social media services.

- **Students**

This is where the students are going. Through here, you can invite students into your classroom and handle their level of permissions. To encourage students to your class, you must set them up in your Google Apps for Education account as Google Contacts, or they must be on the school list.

- **About:**

This is where you will attach the title and summary of the course, attach the class location, and add materials to the Google Drive folder for your study.

- **Add a new class:**

Just as on the Welcome screen, you can create a new class by clicking the plus sign next to your username in the top left corner.

- **Rename or archive a class:**

Press the three dots stacked next to the class name to either rename or archive the file. Archiving a class ensures that while you and your students are still able to access the class, no one is allowed to add assignments or make any other adjustments. Under the Archived portion of the Home menu, the class must pass. But don't worry; you can restore the archived class by browsing Archived Classes at any time, click the three stacked dots, and selecting restore.

- **Use Google Drive for class:**

Tap the file folder icon at the bottom right of the screen. This opens the Google Drive, where all resources in your classroom are stored.

1.3 Users of Google Classroom

Google does not charge for using the Classroom to most students. The real reward is the millions of youth learning how to use their apps. Once these students join the workplace, they will possibly continue to use paid options and even inspire colleagues to follow the devices. Google Classroom was also popular in the U.S. Still, demand is now coming from places with few pre-virus customers, such as Italy and Indonesia, according to Avni Shah, Google's education vice president. Over the last month, all of these places have been lighting up.

The presence of the business in schools started around 2014. A new educational standard, called the Common Core, was gaining momentum in the US and demanding online assessments. Google filled schools with Chrome books, laptops running on the company's Chrome OS. Both were cheaper than Apple Inc. and Microsoft Corp.'s competing phones and came with pre-installed Google apps like Gmail, Docs, Slides, and Drive. Last year, according to researcher Future source, Google controlled 60 percent of the U.S. educational computer market.

Chrome books have been among the first to link to the cloud in classrooms, making it easier for teachers and students to work and keep in touch from anywhere. According to Mike Fisher, an associate director of Future source, that helped spread the adoption.

Likewise, Google Classroom is taking off because it's relatively easy to use and versatile. It is competing with hundreds of other learning-management systems like Canvas and Edmodo that allow schools to upload and track coursework. Classroom synchronizes with specific policies and integrates with other school applications that are already popular, including Google's. And crucially, the app is free for Google, although most rivals are paying money for premium features.

E-learning tool makers rely on platforms such as Classrooms to get into classrooms. Google Classroom is the platform for students to send assignments and teachers to track progress. Jam board, another Google app, helps the teachers to create interactive lessons. Some of the students, as young as 6, have become so talented that they make their videos describing their assignments.

You can use google classroom if you have a G suit, or you are a G suit organization. Mostly the goggle classroom is used by the students, teachers, parents, and the schools.

1. Teachers:

Google has worked with educators nationally to create Classroom: a simplified, easy-to-use resource that helps teachers navigate the coursework. The educators will build classes with Classrooms, allocate tasks, rate and submit reviews, and see all in one place.

How do teachers use Google Classroom?

Since it's a relatively versatile platform, teachers are using its functionality in several different ways. The teachers can use Google Classroom to:

- Streamline how classes are handled. The platform integrates with other tools such as Files, Drive, and Calendar from Google, and there are plenty of built-in "shortcuts" for classroom management tasks. For example, if you update an assignment with a due date, your students will automatically see it added to the class calendar.

- Compile, distribute, and collect assignments, materials for the course, and student research online. Teachers are often able to post an assignment to different classes or to change and repeat assignments year after year. Google Classroom will help you stop any trips to the photocopier and cut down on some of the paper shufflings that come with teaching and learning if your students have daily access to the apps.

- Notify students about their classwork. You can use the website to post announcements and notes about assignments, and it is easy to see who has finished their work or who has not. You may also check-in privately with individual students, answer their questions, and give support.

- Provide proper feedback to the students timely on their assignments and assessments. Google Forms can be used inside Google Classroom to build and exchange quizzes, which are automatically graded as students turn them in. Not only do you spend less time grading, but your students will provide instant input on their work.

Do teachers use Google Classroom as live teaching, as with Zoom?

Usually Not. However, Google offers Hangouts Meet's premium features free to teachers and students who are at home during the coronavirus pandemic, allowing for virtual meetings of up to 250 people as well as live streaming. The recording feature in Hangouts Meet, also, to live video capabilities, gives teachers an easy tool to create pre-recorded lesson videos for students to watch at their own time. With these video tutorials from the Google Teacher Center for Education, teachers can get started with Hangouts Meet.

How can teachers add students to a classroom?

When a classroom has been built, you'll need to enroll your students. There are three choices you have when enrolling your students: Enroll file, add by email, or import from Google Classroom. To enroll students, from your dashboard's main page, pick the classroom you want to add them to, then click on the "Students" tab. Click on Add Students, lastly.

- **Enrolling Code:**

It is the easiest way to enroll your students while they're in the room with you and when you're trying to enroll them.

First, click on "Use Code." A six-digit alphanumeric code that is distinctive to your classroom will be issued.

Then, visit http:/enroll.goguardian.com to have your students enter the code.

Scan the "Students" tab in your classroom from the Teacher dashboard, then press the Enroll button (the little icon on the right-hand side of the student name) to connect the student to the classroom.

- **By email address:**

You may attach students to your Chrome book through email address whether or not they are logged in. To do so, use the option "Add Emails."

Type the email addresses of each student you wish to connect to the classroom in the window that pops up. After typing each email address, tap the ENTER key, then press "Add Students" when you have finished entering the email addresses of all students.

And everybody's sorted!

- **By Code:**

Generating a folder with the email addresses of your students to send to Go Guardian using CSV A CSV or comma-separated value format. See the video on social media for guidance on how to send CSV to students.

Firstly, click on the button, "Import CSV."

Build a CSV file on your machine with one email address per line, and no header row. Then pick this file from the Teacher dashboard by clicking the "Click or drag upload file" button to search and select the file or simply drag and drop the file into that button.

Click on the "Import Students" button to add your students to the session.

- **Inscribe students from Google Classroom:**

If you added classrooms via Google, then your students will be automatically inscribed in your Go Guardian classroom. And, as classrooms can change, you should always update your roster to ensure that all of your students are enrolled correctly. Every hour the list of students enrolled in your classroom is updated. You can also sync manually at any time by any time by pressing the Google Sync Students button.

How do Google Classroom teachers make their students more engaged and interactive?

To make learning more interactive for students with digital content, consider combining the types of tools that you share with them in Google Classroom. Apart from G Suite tools such as Google Docs and Google Slides, teachers and students can share other media forms, including photos, website links, YouTube videos, and screencasts. Some teachers also have a range of choices for students to apply for their work inside Google Classroom. For example, you may give students the option to reply with a comment, video clip, or drawing to a reading assignment that demonstrates their thought.

If you are looking to create an interactive platform for students, you might be considering doing so on the Stream page of Google Classroom. The Stream is a feed inside Google Classroom where everyone in the class will find updates and upcoming assignments, and it is the first thing students see when they log in. Alice Keeler, a well-known blogger who writes thoroughly about Google Classroom, suggests that you use the Stream to post your class plan and recommend that you use Screencast to post student video messages.

Some teachers use the Stream to create class discussion boards, where students can connect online by asking questions or commenting on the posts. Such discussion boards will help improve class engagement and give more leverage to students in getting their voices heard by the class. You can use the Stream as a secure social network of sorts with conversations, and it can be a way to help children practice using

all kinds of different digital citizenship skills in a "walled garden" style environment.

What other Google Classroom applications and websites do they integrate?

Now there are hundreds of external apps and websites which are part of Google Classroom. Some of these apps can partner with Google, while others in the Chrome store build and publish their third-party add-ons. If you are extensively using Google Classroom, the integration of other EdTech tools can be an excellent way to streamline your instruction. For example, you want your students to use Quizlet to learn some vocabulary words; you can use the integration with Google Classroom to share and allocate a similar flashcard collection to your class directly. Or, if you're searching for other online learning material, there's a collaboration with publishers you'll find all kinds of posts, videos, and other educational content to share with your students.

2. Student:

The classroom is free education, non-profit, for anyone with a personal Google Account service. Classroom allows communicating with learners and teachers easy — inside and outside of schools. The classroom saves time and paper and makes designing lessons, assigning tasks, interacting, and keeping organized simple. It is a good option for students who want to learn in their free time.

How does a student set up Google Classroom?

The simple Google Classroom setup method is relatively easy, particularly for first-time users. The Google Teacher Center offers multiple tutorials to get started. If you are in search of the most popular videos and details, this is your best bet. There are also plenty of do-it-yourself tutorials shared by professors and software design professionals on YouTube. Many of these videos produced by teachers provide practical tips and tricks they have learned in their classrooms by using the website.

What is Google doing with students' data? Should you be worried about privacy?

As an educator, safeguarding the privacy and data of your students will undoubtedly be a concern when selecting a multimedia platform for your classroom. Whenever a tool can collect student data, it's essential to ask questions about how the companies involved protect, use, or store student data. For more information, please read our full Google Classroom Privacy Report.

Google says privacy and protection of data is a top priority for all G Suite for Education products. However, educators should bear in mind that there is a right for parents and families to opt-out if they don't want their children using Google products in school. Once Google Classroom is launched, school administrators and teachers may want to have an alternate program in place for students who may opt-out.

Many educators, families, and activists have raised concerns in the past about Google's ability to deliver on privacy and data security commitments. What's more, Google's dominance in branding and school products has raised concerns about the trade-offs that enable Google to develop its brand in schools. If you're using Google Classroom or not, it's essential to get students to think critically about data privacy and the ads we see in different areas of our lives-including our classrooms.

Why is Google Classroom supportive of classroom differentiation?

Google Classroom will help streamline the formative evaluation, which is essential for supporting students who might need further support or additional challenges. For example, you can use this platform to build, distribute, and collect digital exit tickets or auto-graded appraisals quickly. Google Classroom can, in a way, make it easier and faster to gather daily feedback on the progress of your students. There are, of course, plenty of other formative evaluation resources out there, many of which now provide Google Classroom integrations.

Google Classroom also makes it easy for individual students or small groups to customize assignments. It means teachers will give other students or classes in a class changed or different assignments. You also have the opportunity to check-in privately with a student and see if they have questions or need any extra support. The ability to do all of this online may make the distinction efforts of teachers less visible for the class, something that could be beneficial to students who might feel singled out.

Differentiation will still be a matter of innovative problem-solving with or without a device like Google Classroom, and there is no one or "right" way to do that. Fortunately, many teachers post online their ideas, strategies, and innovative solutions.

3. Parents:

It's hard to skip the most popular tools Google has to offer — Gmail, Google Calendar, and Google Docs are all staples to get organized and work done. Such interactive tools have revolutionized how we interact, collaborate, and store information online. The educationally-friendly Google Classroom app brings the benefits of paperless networking and interactive communication to classrooms for teachers and students. Tens of millions of teachers and students in thousands of schools around the world use Google Classroom, making it one of the most common EdTech resources today. Parents can also use google classroom for various purposes; they like to gain information about their children's progress from teachers.

How can Google Classroom keep families and parents in the loop?

Google Classroom has options for teachers to submit classroom notifications; however, it doesn't provide the degree of contact you'll find in resources such as Seesaw, Remind, or ClassDojo. Google introduce to parents and families as "guardians" who may opt to receive summaries of unfinished assignments, upcoming assignments, and other class activity by email. However, it does not include features for direct messaging with families or permits families to comment on the work of their children.

Where can you use Google Classroom to find more ideas?

If you're looking for official Google Classroom stuff, check out the Google Education Twitter feed for product updates, teacher ideas, videos, and even a newsletter about G Suite for Education items. Most fans of Google Classroom are also tweeting, blogging, and even podcasting on all the ways students use the site. For millions of teachers and ed-tech experts doing field research, exploring, and innovating for Google Classroom, fellow educators can quickly find tips and inspiration online.

Should not be afraid to get creative with your tactics, hacks, and imaginative uses for the platform when you're using Google Classroom.

Here are some smart ways to use google classroom

This may lack the visual appeal of iPads or the prestige of a BYOD system for students. It may not be as forward-thinking as we would like here at Teach Thinking. Still, Google Classroom excels in offering options for a wide range of teachers who have a variety of experience and level of familiarity with the technology of education. It also uses the popular Google template used by many teachers for years. As such, it scratches the itch for teachers right now, in many classrooms.

So below are things you can do with Google Classroom, at least. When new ideas come in, the platform evolves, and we know more about its subtleties on our own, we'll be reviewing this list.

- When a task, lecture, or unit is not working, add your comments – or let students give their feedback), then tag it or save it for revision to a specific tab.
- Align resume with other teachers.
- Share data with a group of qualified learners.

- Hold copy written samples for preparation.
- Embellish your resume.
- Using Google Forms to seek regular, weekly, by-semester, or yearly input from students and parents.
- Share anonymous excerpts of students' teaching.
- See how the tasks turn out from the students.
- Flip the classroom open. Google Apps for Education has at its heart the tools for publishing videos and posting assignments.
- Communicate with students about task requirements.
- Let the students pose in private questions.
- Let students create their own, their favorite jobs, digital portfolios.
- We are creating a list of accepted sources of study. You may distinguish this also by the student, school, level of reading, and more.
- For students or students and parents, post an announcement.
- For your students, develop more mobile learning experiences – in higher-end, for example.
- Let students use Google Sheets to map their development over time.
- Share due dates with mentors who have a public calendar outside the classroom.
- Students communicate separately, or as groups. Better still, watch how they interact with each other.
- Using Google Forms to create a test that grades to itself.
- Check file rights (view, edit, copy, download), file by file.

- Let students curate artifacts of project-based learning.
- You will work with other teachers as a group (same grade by the team, the same material through grade levels).
- Encourage digital citizenship through recorded peer-to-peer interaction.
- Using Google Calendar for due dates, out-of-class events, and other significant "chronological details."
- Digitally interact with students who might refuse to 'speak' to you in person.
- Streamline with other teachers the cross-curricular programs.
- Collect and publish frequently visited websites to ensure that they all have the same access, the corresponding data, the same links, and the same information.
- They are learning the student vertically aligned by curating and sharing "landmark" student assignments that demonstrate mastery of common standards.
- Encourage a shared language by eliminating expectations and district-wide sharing.
- Encourage the students to use their smartphones to study formally. Students will have an opportunity to see their phone as something more than a mere entertainment tool by viewing documents, YouTube channels, community contact, digital portfolio pieces, and more on a BYOD app.
- Develop and publish the 'control principles' for accountability and cooperation (with students, other teachers, and other schools).
- Promote relationships between peer-to-peer and school-to-school – students with other students, students with other teachers, and teachers with other teachers.

- For example, build 'by-need' groups as classes—based on the level of reading.
- Test what assignments students have received.
- Provide reviews to graduates.
- Add the student writing voice comments (this includes a third-party app to do so).
- Help the students create YouTube channels unique to content.
- Annotated research papers 'Closed-circuit Publish' according to different styles (MLA, APA, etc.) or otherwise 'confusing' work.
- Share introductions.
- For questions, build a digital parking lot".'
- Administer slips for the wireless exit.
- Allocate volunteer 'lesson extensions' to students rather than homework. Refer to who has accessed and accomplished what, and when questions arise about mastery or grades.
- Develop folders of miscellaneous materials from classes. Digital Text Versions, etc. 44. Enjoy better conferencing with readily available work for students and parents, info, writing, reviews, access data, and so on.
- Store pdfs or other digital assets snapshots into universally accessible files.
- Build a wall of data but with speed sheets and color-coding.
- Easily access sub-working or make-up jobs.

- Gather info. This can happen in several ways, including using Google Forms, Google Sheets extraction, or your in-house process.
- Learn how to send quick reviews.
- See who got what – and when – at-a-glance done.
- Track when students are turning in to work.
- Because access is tracked, look for patterns in student habits – those who instantly access assignments, those who regularly return to work, and so on – and communicate those trends to students (anonymously) as a way to convey "best practices in learning" for students who might not otherwise think
- Differentiate training by tiring, grouping, or spiraling up Bloom.
- Develop classes that are based on ability, interest, reading level, or other teaching and learning factors.
- Using Google Forms to poll students, build surveys on reader interest, and more.
- Layout a list with cited works.
- Build datasheets.
- Digital team-building concept.
- Build a paperless classroom.
- Share common and regularly accessed assignments – project instructions, year-long due dates, math formulas, information about the subject field, historical timelines, etc.

1.4 Google Classroom for Elementary Grades

For many teachers, distance learning is new. When we had technology in our classes, we got direct input from students as to whether the technology worked or not, and whether the task was satisfactory to them.

A lot of teachers use Google Classroom for Distance Learning. Some teachers are new to the site and have it just set up. Many teachers need some organizational advice, and others have long been using the website.

We all know our time at school is very tight. We are just not getting enough of that. Planning, data collection, grading. There is not enough time to get anything done. Yet you too can be a great teacher with a little support from Google Classroom, and keep coordinated.

We do use Google Classroom in your classes. It's an educational resource inside Google Apps designed to help teachers build and collect paperless classwork! Sure, you heard about this. NO MORE TO GRADE PILES! Once you set it all up, it generates Google Drive files for each project, which helps to keep everyone coordinated for each test.

To build a Google Classroom account, you would need to sign up first. When you have set up an account, you can create a page for your students only! This is your page in Google Classroom! To build a new site Google Classroom, click on the + symbol.

Once you have named your class, it will generate a class code that will allow your students to "enter" the class. Only your students can display or post material to your classroom page this way. It was super quick, and it took only around 1-2 mints to enter.

There will be four features on your Home page: Source, CLASSWORK, Men, and GRADES. When you have typed in the hidden class code for your students, you can see their names listed under the PEOPLE tab. One nice feature is the students' ability to comment and post on their Facebook page. You simply press CLASSWORK and CREATE to start making tasks, quizzes, or posts for your students. You then have the choice to call it, add a description or instructions, and assign a due date.

You then have the option to add a file from your Google Drive or device, a connection, or even an instructional or educational video! Classroom Flipped, anybody?

One fantastic feature is the ability to select which form of access to this new file you want your students to have. Students can only display what's perfect for handouts or things you only want your students to learn. They can also edit the file, ensuring ALL the students will be able to access the same folder and edit the same document. Finally, a copy can be produced for each student through Google Classroom. Now every kid has his paper. You can also further distinguish and delegate those assignments to specific students.

In Google Classroom, students will transform anything in an assignment. No longer have to "share" a Google Doc with you and clutter your alerts inbox. You will see who made it into the task and who didn't work on the task and still does.

After they have turned in an assignment, you can rate it, offer input or suggestions, and send it back to them to review and update their score or make any required adjustments to their assignment.

Using this method has helped save me loads of time and my wellbeing. Google Classroom is a simple and easy way to give students assignments, and without all the needless paperwork, they can complete and turn them into. Google classroom is ideal for all students, and elementary grades can use Google classroom as well.

Chapter 2: Benefits and Features of Google Classroom

Google Classroom is a free program for teachers and learners to collaborate. Teachers can create classes online, invite students to attend the class, and create and hand out assignments. Inside the forum, learners and teachers can interact with the assignments, and teachers can track the progress of students. To use this solution, schools can create a free Google Apps for Education account.

Google Classroom offers teachers and students special features that are not part of regular Google Accounts. For example, teachers may use the Formulas tool to add images and answers to questions with multiple choices. The Gmail Inbox app houses Classroom messages, allowing students and teachers to find highlights and primary information with ease. By adding subjects to posts, teachers can organize their class streams, and students and teachers can search the streams to find different subjects.

Google Classroom is perfect for parents too. Teachers can exchange student success summaries with their parents, and the latter can get automatic email summaries of class updates and student assignments. In this chapter, we discuss how much you benefit from the google classroom and how you can take advantage of its features.

2.1 Advantages of Google Classroom

Google Classroom offers teachers a range of distinct advantages, but college students and even designers may also benefit from this. Recent years have seen paperless classrooms becoming more common than ever. Students now complete the majority of their research online, including in rural areas and at several universities. This move saves a toll on the environment by cutting back on paper use, and it's also convenient for students, particularly those who may not have access to an actual classroom but are digitally attending.

Google's classroom was launched in the summer of 2014 and is now being used in schools across the US. Google Classroom provides many opportunities for both students and teachers as a free online learning site. Below are the reasons teachers should try it out.

- **Accessibility:**

Google Classroom can be operated from any computer through Google Chrome or from any mobile device, whatever the platform. All files shared by teachers and students are stored on Google Drive in a Classroom folder. Users can access the Classroom anywhere, anywhere. Students can't complain about broken machines or starving dogs anymore.

- **Exposure:**

The classroom offers an online learning framework for students. Many programs at the college and university now allow students to participate in at least one online class. Google Classroom exposure can help students turn to other learning management systems used in higher education.

- **Paperless**

Teachers and students don't have to move unnecessary quantities of paper because the Classroom is paperless. When teachers upload assignments and evaluations to the Classroom, they are saved to drive simultaneously. Students can complete assignments and assessments directly from the Classroom, and even keep their work to Drive. Students can access missing work due to absences and find other services that may be required.

The stacks of papers are high. Trust me, when you no longer hold the huge teacher bag everywhere, your back will thank you. You know, the one that blends so beautifully into all your stacks of paper. If the stacks of paper are your thing, that's cool. But I'm sure you would think it's an even better idea not to have paper stacks. Don't worry; all those binder clips will still find plenty of uses.

- **Time Saver:**

The classroom is an incredible time-saver. With all money being saved in one location and being able to access the Classroom anytime, teachers would have more free time to complete other tasks. As the Classroom is accessible from a mobile device, teachers and students can participate through their phones or tablets.

All the tools for a class are in a single location for the students. You don't need to find a book, grab your pad, drive to a lecture room, or print an essay. Instead, you can view the lesson online, answer questions, and even apply all of the work in one place. This way, everything stays clean and ordered, and time is not wasted in search of missing materials for classroom use.

All the students, records, applications, and grades are at one convenient location for teachers.

- **Communication:**

Built-in devices make it a breeze to connect with parents and students. Teachers and students can submit emails, post into the web, submit private comments on assignments, and provide input on work. Teachers are in complete charge of comments and updates from the students. They can also connect with parents via individual emails or via email summaries from the Classroom that include class announcements and dates.

- **Collaborate:**

The classroom gives students several ways to collaborate. Teachers will encourage online conversations inside the Classroom between students and create group projects. Additionally, students can collaborate on teacher shared Google Docs.

- **Engagement:**

Many digital natives are technically confident and would be more likely to take control of their learning utilizing technology. The classroom provides many ways to make learning collaborative and interactive. This allows teachers to separate assignments, to incorporate videos and web pages into lessons, and to create group assignments for collaboration.

- **Differentiation:**

Through Classroom, teachers may easily distinguish learner instruction. Assigning lessons to the entire class, individual students, or student groups only takes a few basic steps when making an assignment on the Classwork website.

- **Feedback:**

Giving students meaningful feedback is a valuable part of all learning. Within the Classroom's grading tool, teachers can send feedback on assignments to each student. There's also the opportunity to build a comment bank for future use inside the grading method. Furthermore, the iOS device Classroom helps users to annotate research.

- **Data Analysis:**

To render learning meaningful, teachers will evaluate data from tests and ensure that students recognize learning goals.

Data from evaluations can be conveniently exported for sorting and analyzing into Sheets.

- **Take advantage of an Easy-to-Use Tool:**

Google Classroom provides a highly intuitive, super easy-to-learn GUI. Through each step of the process, the platform talks to you. You'll be asked to "communicate with your class here" when you land on the main page of your classroom. You can make announcements and schedule them to go out at your own time. Additionally, you can answer any student questions. The GUI is also self-explanatory, which means the use of the app does not have a learning curve.

- **It is easy to integrate with Other Google Products**

Google Classroom with Google Docs, Sheets, and Slides. Offering a platform that syncs with other free tools for schools on a tight budget provides a way for schools and students to get into the 20th century without spending a fortune on costly classroom software.

Teachers have assignments, and students interpret them as jobs. The student crosses that off once the work is done. A formal collection of task completion steps keeps everyone focused and helps to avoid confusion about the tasks that are due to them.

- **Allow Students to Interact with Other Students**

One function of Google Classroom is the development of tasks, like questions. You can use set up how many points a topic is worth and even let students interact. A website that is easy to access, even in an online environment, encourages interaction and enables students to learn from each other.

Besides the students interacting with each other, the instructor can communicate via email with individual students, and even with parents, posts to a network, private comments, and feedback. You can make a class announcement that implements to all registered students.

- **Learn how to use an Online Learning Platform:**

Many colleges are already using a mix of learning environments online and in real life. Using Google Classroom gives you experience with either an instructor or a student in an online environment.

You can sign in as a student if you're an instructor and check how the platform works so you can direct any confused students a bit. As the world is increasingly linked, even for topics like graphic design, where students can now view a lesson online and upload work through a whiteboard or attachment, expect even more online courses.

- **Provide Video Lessons:**

YouTube is an easy platform to use, and Google Classroom enables you to either insert a video produced by someone else on a theme, or build your video, and upload the embed code through URL.

Video lessons feature you to compete with some of the more competitive sites that charge monthly rates for similar functions in a classroom. However, you can add videos at no charge with Google Classroom, and even split them into topics.

- **Add New Students Quickly:**

Attach new students to Google Classroom quickly. Only navigate to tag "Men." You can see a list of teachers and students with a symbol for a little child and a sign for plus to the right. To add another teacher and share some of the workloads, or allow someone to take over your class, click on the individual icon next to the word "Teachers."

Students may also add to your class if you give them the code that's put just below the student's list.

- **Distinguish Between Skill Levels:**

If you have more than one ability level in a classroom, Google Classroom enables you to distinguish by setting up as many different classrooms as you like. One example of this may be self-guided read programs. You may have two or three student classes using the system, but group A may be at 6th-grade reading level, group B at 4th-grade reading level, and group C at 2nd grade reading.

With Google Classroom, you can split each group, so they work at their speed, but you can still see all of your students from the same dashboard and coordinate who's working on what to keep on top of who needs additional support. and who's excelling in the topic and who needs more of a challenge.

- **Cut the Excuses:**

Several students seem to have a reason for not handing in their work forever. You've heard the old response of "the dog ate my homework," but some students are taking excuses to a new level. Work is graded and submitted online in a digital classroom, which ensures it can't be "lost." Digital systems often allow parents to keep on top of what their students completed and what still needs to be done.

Some schools often use online learning on snow days, rather than requiring students to make cancellations because of extreme weather. After it would have finished, spring break is no longer cut through or school in session for a week after. Instead, the school offers access to online learning programs so that even on days when school doesn't, work continues.

- **Easy Workflow Management:**

Say goodbye to alphabetically gathering tasks or checking the names off a chart. For Google Classroom, you'll be able to keep track of tasks that have come in. It makes it easy to know the status of everyone and to follow up with students who neglect research. All are time-stamped, and it's easy to spot late work.

- **See Real-Time Progress**

Google Classroom makes it simple for students to check in on the research. Tap on a thumbnail of any student's assignment from the Student Work page to show real-time progress. From there, the comment feature in Docs or Slides can be used to provide direct input. To monitor changes since your last view, use the handy revision history feature. The history of revision also helps you to see how productive (or not so productive) a single student was during class time.

- **Work Is Never Lost:**

Because Google Apps are cloud-based, implying that they reside on the Internet rather than on your hard drive. Google Classroom work saves instantly and is available from any computer. Students can operate smoothly wherever they are, without thinking about clunky flash drives, sending back and forth email files or losing progress due to device malfunction. "I left it at home," and "My machine crashed before I was able to recover," is no longer an excuse to entertain.

- **There's An App For That:**

With the software, students and teachers may experience all of Google Classroom's features on a mobile device. When assignments and announcements are posted, students receive notifications on their phones, making it easy for students to stay at the top of classroom happenings. As an instructor, the app allows you to post from your phone — either directly from the app, or use share-sheet support (that little sharing icon you click while posting images or websites from your computer). Can't get any more relaxed than this.

- **Need A Copy On Extra? View Google Classroom.**

Stop thinking about keeping track of additional copies. Upload resources from your unit to Google Classroom, and then let students take control. And when students come to you to ask for those two-week-old assignments they skipped, you can just guide them to Google Classroom. It's also an excellent place to post rubrics, checklists, and other resources frequently cited by the students.

- **View All Work By A Single Student On One Screen:**

Teachers may also display a single list of the entire year's work for increasing students. This ensures that any student can have convenient access to all the research during the year ideal for student- or parent-teacher conferences, children's studies, IEP meetings, and more.

- **Ask Questions And Encourage Online Discussions:**

Using the function "Build Query" to add a query to the stream in the classroom. You can set it to private, so you can only see the responses, or allow the students to respond to each other.

- **Keep Families Informed:**

Guardian Summaries will give families a weekly rundown of your classroom route, including announcements and due dates for the assignment. If some research is lacking from a student, it will be shown too.

- **Differentiate Like A Boss:**

Once an assignment is made, teachers have the option to submit it to the entire class or individual students. This ensures that you can quickly discern orders, products, and due dates without having to pick out anyone.

- **It's Always Improving:**

Google is serious regarding feedback. Google Classroom is already a great resource, but it is continually improving based on its users' feedback. You can provide feedback at any time by clicking on the small question mark at the bottom left of the screen

- **Google Classroom is easy to use**

Relative to other common LMS (Learning Management Systems) in the last decade, Google Classroom is incredibly simple. It doesn't take more time or expertise to create a new classroom. Tech team practiced for about an hour, by the end of the training, and had all set up and run a classroom.

- **Google Classroom lets you connect more effectively**

You only enter the students' email addresses once, and the classroom contact is finished. The instructor only has an email address, a discussion group, and automatically created a Google Calendar by joining the student in the classroom. And adding and removing students from class as needed is simple.

- **Google Classroom lets you interact more effectively**

Even more relevant than being user-friendly and secure, communication tools are also quite powerful. Since it's all Cloud-based, students no longer "lose" assignments. The contact is smooth when a student is absent. Google Classroom only last month introduced a parent feedback feature to keep parents updated on what's happening in the "classroom."

- **Google Classroom is more cost-effective and environmentally friendly**

Because every student already has a laptop that links to the Internet, every piece of paper we save just makes the school more productive and environmentally conscious.

- **To students who struggle**

As long as you help them handle the tool, it is best. (The computer itself can also be a nuisance, so handling that needs to be taught.) The reason Google Classroom is stronger is because of its organizational advantage. Tasks never get lost, and the teacher is already planning every classroom. Navigating this has to be taught for these students. Although students are digital natives, this does not mean they understand how adults are arranging their environment to help them learn.

- **Collaboration is simpler with Google Classroom outside of the school**

(i.e., Flipped Classroom). Again, with a link, it is Cloud-based and available from anywhere. Students are permitted to share assignments and work together from home to complete them. Collaboration isn't all about interacting with other peers in a group. By sharing a video, a teacher will flip the classroom to go live in the evening, allowing students to watch it that night to practice for a quiz on it the next day. The possibilities are endless.

- **Teacher preparation is simple, and upfront time is worth it**

Newer functionality in Google Classroom will allow teachers to schedule future tasks. Designated assignments could go live on a given date. When an instructor has a lengthy absence, you can organize the tasks and do not need to rely on others to manage it. Classrooms are also available from semester to semester and from year to year. Copying and pasting a lesson for the next group of students would be awful for an instructor, but it saves some time to have some items already in place (class syllabus, grading standards, etc.).

- **Feedback is instantaneous and accessible by embedding forms**

This improves interaction and transparency, which helps the instructor to see results at the end of the lesson, too. If students failed to reply with the correct answers, she could then cover the material again.

- **Updates are a constant**

If you need to changed or correct things, Google listens and reacts (from this came both the timing of the assignment and the parent communication). That also means teachers will have to keep learning while they use it, which is not a bad thing either!

- **Using Google's Proven Technology Expertise:**

Google Classroom is part of both Google Apps, and the Google ecosystem developed. This approach, therefore, allows good use of Google's proven technical infrastructure and interconnectivity to provide users with a top-rate education approach.

- **Advantages for Teachers:**

Teachers may easily build online courses to supplement the other courses they are conducting. They will exchange learning resources with their students, and these can be easily accessed and downloaded. Additionally, educators can build assignments online and also monitor the progress and success of students in assignments.

- **Advantages for Students**

Students may quickly access their educator's assignments and learning materials. They can also use the forum to communicate with the instructor and other students whenever they want. Google Drive and Docs interconnectivity enable students to apply completed assignments like rich media.

- **Part of Google for Education**

Google Classroom is part of the Google Education Suite, which includes Gmail, Drive, Hangouts, Pages, Slides, Forms, Papers, Documents, Vault, and Calendar. Classroom Software is only open to educators. Schools can receive an email in their domain, and the software is ad-free. Finally, Google offers free e-mail and ticket support for all users.

To summarize, Google Classroom links teachers with students makes it easy to create an online class and invite learners. Allows teachers to allocate assignments, encourages discussions between students and teachers, allows teachers to review and rate assignments, and allows students to display class materials, documents, and assists.

2.2 Google Classroom Features and Educational App

The classroom is a free suite of collaboration tools with email, documents, and storage included. The classroom has been developed in partnership with teachers to help them save time, coordinate classes, and enhance communication with students.

Want to stick to the Classroom? Check out what's new in the Classroom to stay up-to-date with feature updates, follow Google Education on Twitter, and subscribe to the Google Education page.

Although we love Apple's goods, device ecology, and general aesthetics at Teach Thought, we prefer to recommend Google for most classrooms. While they're not mutually exclusive, the classroom that has the Chrome books and iPads budget is unusual. 1:1 is still rare; 2:1 is even more unique.

Google Classroom is the product of bundling Google's Google Calendar, Google Drive, Gmail, and other resources into something that teachers can use more comfortable. We showed you the uses of google classroom in the last chapter, and now we'll tell you the classroom features.

1. Drag & Drop on Classwork Page:

We rolled out the new Classwork page last fall, where instructors can stay organized and chart their classes. Yet, we know teachers organize their courses in various ways and require more versatility in their resources in the classroom. So now you can drag and drop whole topics and specific things in the Classwork, quickly rearranging them on the list. On the Classwork tab, you can drag an entire subject to a particular spot, or drag specific things into — and in between — themes. This feature launched on mobile last year, and now it's time for it to hit the internet.

2. Refreshed Ux:

Beginning today (January 2019), you'll also see that the Classroom has a new look and feel, first on the site, and then on the smartphone devices throughout the classroom. We launched Google's latest content theme back in 2014 to provide greater consistency across Google's products and platforms. You'll see a more fluid style flow among the changes — plus a modern approach to form, color, iconography, and typography on both the web and the mobile app. We also make the class code easier to access and project so that students can find and enter quickly. And finally, we launch 78 new themes with design illustrations, ranging from history to math to hairdressing to photography. Now, more than ever, you can personalize your Classroom.

3. Updated Preparation & Support

The need for more help arises with new resources and improvements. In the Teacher Center, you can find modified videos with the latest design and functionality that we rolled out in 2018 on the First Day of Classroom Training. We created a new and enhanced Support Center while we're at it, in conjunction with our Group and product platform.

4. Questions to Post:

You may post questions to your classroom and enable the students to have discussions by answering each other's answers (not, depending on the setting you choose). You can post a video, for example, and ask students to answer a question related to this, or post an article and ask them to write something in response.

5. Reuse Assignments:

If you reuse your curricula year after year – or at least reuse your papers, you may want an upgrade. Now you can repeat assignments, announcements, or questions from all of your classes or from any class you co-teach, be it from last year or last week. When you pick what you want to copy, you'll also be able to make adjustments before publishing or assigning them.

6. Enhanced Application Calendar

We appreciate corrections to boost workflow. The classroom will automatically create a calendar in Google Calendar for each of your classes over the next month. All tasks that have a due date will be added to your class calendar automatically and held up to date. Within the Classroom or on Google Calendar, you will be able to display your schedule where you can manually add class activities such as field trips or guest speakers.

7. Bump a post:

Sticking to blog articles, tweets, or Facebook notifications has become a thing of the past. Now you can even do it on Google Classroom by pushing every post upwards.

8. Optional:

If you're using long-term projects or other tasks with no due date, you can now build tasks in Google Classroom without due dates.

9. Add a Google Form to a post:

If you're a Google fan, you'll appreciate this shift. A lot of teachers used Google Forms as a simple way to give the class an exam, quiz, or survey. Teachers and students will be able to add Google Forms from Drive to posts and assignments coming in the next few weeks and get a connection in the Classroom to show the answers quickly.

10. YouTube Functionality

Love YouTube, but is it about the objectionable material? Google listens. As it also includes content that an organization or school does not find suitable, we introduced advanced YouTube settings as an Additional Feature last month for all Google Apps domains. These settings allow Apps to admins the ability to limit the viewable YouTube videos for signed-in users, as well as users who are signed-out on admin-managed networks.

11. Communicate and collaborate

- Connect anywhere — Enable Classroom 24/7 on the internet or via mobile devices throughout the Android and iOS Classroom.

- Real-time feedback — In the Docs grading tool, view, comment, and edit student work in real-time. The student annotates research in the mobile device Classroom.

- Create class discussions — On the Stream tab, post announcements, involve students in question-driven discussions, invite students to respond to classmates, and push essential topics up.

- Handle class discussions — Control who can post to the Stream list, and discourage individual students from posting or commenting.

- Share content — Share photos, videos, and pictures from Classroom websites with one click in the Share to Classroom extension.

- Transfer content to screens for students — Send sites to a class with the Share to Classroom extension instantly. Students will share their computers with their teachers, as well.

- Communicate with guardians — Teachers in any G Suite domain that invite parents and guardians to sign up for email summaries, which include upcoming or missed work for the student.

12. Comfortable support for administrators:

- Safe and accessible — like every other free G Suite for Education service, the Classroom will not include ads and never uses the material or student data for advertising.

- One sign-in — Teachers and students with their G Suite for Education accounts will sign in to the Classroom.

- Set permissions — Enable or disable Classroom for all users, unique organizational units, and individual school districts of G Suite for Education. Find out which teachers can build and handle classes too.

- Integration of SIS — Use the Classroom API to develop classes and student rosters based on your SIS. If you participate in the beta program, you can also move the grades directly from the Classroom to your student information system (SIS).

- Career Development — Rapid use of Classroom for the teachers with our free online training at the Google Learning Centre.

- 24/7 help free — Find feedback and assistance through the Google Classroom Support Group, the Classroom Help Center or the 24/7 support line.

- Personal data protection — Google Classroom is protected by the 1974 Family Educational Rights and Privacy Act (FERPA) compliance center of the G Suite for Education Terms of Service. Admins can determine whether domain users may grant third party applications access to their Classroom data.

- User analytics in the classroom — Administrators will display Classroom utilization reports in the Admin console.

The best apps for your Google Classroom:

With a connection to the website or page, you can attach virtually anything to Google Classroom. At the same time, this does not require students to work with the software interactively, on the applications. Google Classroom has a lot of apps that have a built-in sharing feature. Students can thus easily open the app via Google Classroom.

Here's what you can do:

1. Build an account inside the App or Website.
2. Build an activity or tool inside the program or web site for your students.
3. Use the option "transfer to Classroom." You can find the option in the application somewhere.
4. Now you can do stuff like create a quiz, and allocate it in one of your classes to your students.

Here are the number of apps you can use for your google classroom

1. Book Widgets:

With Book Widgets (Google for Education Partner), you can build interactive activities on tablets, computers, and smartphones for your students. As an instructor, you can choose from over 40 different games and exercises.

That is so simple! Students use their iPad, Chrome book or smartphone to open the exercise using a special shortcode or to scan the QR code you gave them. Or, in Google Classroom immediately, you can only give them a Book Widgets exercise. Simply download the Chrome plugin Book Widgets and get started in Google Classroom.

With the Live widget feature, you can also follow the operation of your students, live, from a distance, inside Google Classroom.

Book Widgets' greatest benefit is that it's so diverse. Create your worksheets or quizzes? Widgets Book! Do you make your games, such as crossword puzzles, memory, spot the difference, puzzles, etc.? Go and check it now.

2. EDPuzzle:

EDpuzzle is a simple and effective way to deliver videos in your classroom (Google). And it is not just a distributor of videos, Gets to life with EDpuzzle video. Connect audio-notes and video questions.

EDpuzzle makes adding comments to videos simple, and the questions make the video interactive. How do you use EDpuzzle? When students watch a video, you can use it to encourage critical thinking. It is perfect for flipped classrooms, too.

3. Buncee:

Buncee is a design and presentation platform that allows creating material for all classroom purposes simple for you and your students. You can make an excellent presentation, an interactive novel, an entertaining lesson, or a lovely card. Buncee has a lot of fun and interactive media tools and graphics that make it more visual and enjoyable to present.

In Google Classroom, add a slideshow, made with buncee, to your class materials. Students will visit and use the presentation to review a test, or do homework.

4. Nearpod:

Nearpod is likewise a Buncee presentation device. It is a lot more than that too! Build your interactive introductions. Attach some slides, slide by slide, or pick a specific Sway template that you can change.

All of those slides make a great interactive presentation. Especially when you're adding activities such as quizzes, open-ended questions, surveys, questions are drawing, and others. Inside your talk, what about taking your students on a field trip? Only add a slide from Nearpod's library featuring a virtual reality experience.

When your presentation is done, your students can choose to enter a code in their Nearpod app or just click on the connection in Google Classroom assigned to them. You, as an instructor, are in charge of the display. The display on your students' computers will also turn to that slide when you move to another slide.

If your students have to do a quiz or questionnaire, they should do it on their computer, as its part of the presentation. A live set of responses! So, you can see what your students react immediately.

5. Screencastify:

If you want to give clear guidance online, allowing students the ability to process learning material at their speed, you can use Screencastify to record your screen, voice, and yourself when providing guidance and guiding students through some learning material from a distance. Think of homework, or whether certain students need homeschooling and you're teaching them from a Google Classroom distance.

Screencastify makes the development of instruction videos super-easy. Simply install your Chrome browser's Screencastify app, and start making videos by recording your screen and voice. Students will follow through on-screen steps when listening to your comments. Upon completion, save and import the video and share it in your learning environment (e.g., Google Classroom) with your students.

6. Newsela:

Newsela develops an understanding of reading through graded papers, real-time evaluations, and observations that can be applied. Students can read papers at their rates. Newsela delivers stories on 5 adaptive read rates from world-class news publications. Embedded tests such as quizzes can also unlock improvement.

7. Quizlet:

Quizlet is basically a quiz tool that focuses on concepts and words. You add a class as a coach and take a quiz. Share this quiz with only a few clicks on your Google Classroom.

They just have to click on the Google Classroom assignment and select which game they want to play in. They can take a test, select the learning mode, learn by flashcards or match words to their meanings.

Quizlet Live helps the students to work together to find the right term or meaning for the description. It is designed for the analysis of descriptions and terms.

There's a tough thing, though: you can't see what your teammates are saying. If anyone makes a mistake on your squad, you need to start over again. Teams are challenging each other to be the first team to cross the finish line.

Install the Chrome Share to Classroom extension:

Teachers and students who use Chrome browsers can share their web pages with the Chrome Share to Classroom extension. Teachers may also use the extension to build announcements and assignments.

Who can have the extension installed?

- G Suite account administrators — administrators may pre-install an extension for representatives of their organizations. This saves time, eliminates demands for troubleshooting, and means teachers and students can get started with the extension immediately.

- Teachers — you should add the Chrome extension Share to Classroom.
- Students — the extension can also be installed if the teacher gives post-installation instructions to the students.

Installation instructions — administrators:

Only G Suite for Administrators of Education will pre-install the extension for members of their organizations.

1. Log in to the Google Admin console.
2. Click System Control from the Dashboard.
3. Tap User Settings to Handle Chrome.
4. Select the settings for the organizational unit you want to customize.
5. Choose the top-level unit if you want to customize settings for everyone in the organizational structure. Or, pick one of the organization's child units.
6. Tap Control forced-loaded apps at Apps and Extensions and next to Force loaded

Apps and Extensions.

Click Check for Chrome Web Store by name Share to Classroom or code. Click Add Save next to the extension.

Instructions for Teachers:

1. Setup Go to Classroom g.co/share to.
2. Tap On Chrome Add.
3. Tap on Extension Add.

4. To open the extension, press the Share to Classroom button.

Posting instructions for students:

As an instructor, you may post the instructions for installation to the students.

- Click on the connection below:
- Select a class by pressing Pick.
- Click the Choose action to pick the form of a message.
- Click on one option:
  - Build an assignment
  - Ask question
  - Make notification
- Click to go.

As a student, if the instructor posted instructions in the course stream, you can install the Share to Classroom extension.

1. Go to the classroom.google.com.
2. . Click on the link.
3. Tap on the Link to Classroom posting-Chrome Web Store.
4. Tap On Chrome Add.
5. Tap on Extension Add.
6. To open the extension, press the Share to Classroom button.

Troubleshooting:

- Can't reach the Chrome Web Store
- Add Connect to Allowed Apps to the Classroom extension
- "Added to Chrome" error message

- "Not signed in" or "Can't link" error messages

How to use the Google Classroom Mobile Device:

Google Classroom has a device that can be downloaded to your smartphone or tablet for both Android and iOS. You can do some of the things you can do with it through a web browser, but not all. As an instructor, you can find the app very restricting. Here's the lowdown on what the app can and can't do and get started.

Start with the mobile app:

Needless to say. First, you have to install and download the software from either Google Play for Android or the iOS app store. Then start the app, and follow the following steps:

- Tap Sign In at the bottom of the page, on the Welcome tab.

- If you already set up Google Accounts, you will see those. A default Google account isn't going to work with Google Classroom, though. You need to log in to your Education account on Google Apps. Tap Add another account, then.

- Tap There.

- Type the login credentials in your Google Apps for School, then press the right triangle.

- Tap OK in the dialog box on Terms of Service.

- Google demands that you update to Google+. Tap Not Yet for now.

- Google then asks if you'd like to stay up to date with Google's news and deals. Check or uncheck the tab, whichever you prefer, and press the right triangle.

- Google tells you it's signed in to your account with progress. You may select which types of data are synced to your computer on that screen. Best to try them out. Tap the triangle on top.

- In Step 2, you return to the Google Accounts list. Tap the Education account you have just added to Google Apps.

- Google will show you some introductory slides that show Classroom's benefits. Move them in, or press Skip.

You're now logged in, so you can access your Google Classroom account.

What do you do with the Google Classroom smartphone app?

When you open and sign in to the app, you can see your class list in the same way as you might in a web browser. Here's what you can do as a teacher:

- Build or enter a class.

- Make announcements and write notes about assignments.

- Send Students emails.

- Sign in to your Google Drive account.

- Check whether or not the students have completed their assignments.

- Reset your class code or disable it.

What's the mobile app you probe won't do?

Sadly, like other smartphone versions of web applications, the Google Classroom app doesn't do several of the main stuff you need to do as an instructor. Here's a rundown of what you can't do with the app:

- Build an assignment, but students can complete assignments in the app and turn them in.

- Assignments by the school.

- Alter class settings.

- Preserve the stored courses or display them.

Google does state the software is continually improving, so these features can appear at a later date. The best thing about the app is to have input, request these apps, and let Google know you want them.

2.3 Hurdles While Using Google Classroom

What stops the schools from making full use of technology? An informal survey identified the key obstacles: lack of time, followed by lack of vision, poor staff growth, fear, and power. An emerging barrier among students is that "school is blocking all the fun stuff! "They discussed instant messaging, podcasting, and blogging.

Many educators often fear that for the majority, the innovative use of technology is trumped by network security and the risk of abuse by a few students. For example: "We can't use Skype [a system that enables users to make free internet calls to someone who also uses it] to let students debate anyone around the world, because we would be bringing them in viruses." "We can't use podcast language lessons because we don't have the bandwidth." "We need to filter student blogging because they're going to abuse the control."

- **Vision And Time:**

Both of us understand that time is the most valued teacher tool. Yet does "lack of time" mean "It is not our leader's priority"?

Time availability is a function of vision and leadership. Does your district have a strong and compelling idea of why technology is essential? So many programs aim to offer teachers who have just returned from staff development training skills to the students.

But, by the time they graduate, many of the technical expertise we teach students today will be outdated. A vision can be supported by technology, but it cannot be the vision. We know firsthand that at this moment in economic history, many students are not globally competitive because research can immediately spill over the Internet to anyone, anywhere that can offer better or cheaper services and goods. Our country has never before faced this sort of global competition — and it's just beginning.

Children need three essential skills to compete in the worldwide economy, and technology is critical to them all. The advanced research skills and expertise in interpreting information, comprehensive communication expertise, and work habits. Contribute to learners becoming self-directed, self-assessing, and fearless.

Too many of our schools continue to have traditional industrial culture creating a dependence on the learner to be taught. Bolting technology into this culture won't prepare children to be competitive globally.

We need to change the culture instead of teaching students how to be taught to teach them how to be responsible for their learning. We have to prepare our students for the possibility of losing their careers to global competition and continuously reshaping their skills.

- **Techno centric Control Versus Creativity:**

Right as we need to train our students to interact with people around the world, some schools are more worried about network protection than about extending the learning boundaries. For most schools, paper remains the primary development device. Too many machines are, in turn, being used as pencils worth $2,000. Our curriculum remains primarily delivered through textbooks, which can only be revised once every five years in some states.

The actual revolution, however, is about knowledge and communication. Hardware is nothing more than computer plumbing. We do not need Directors of Technology; we need facilitators of information and communication. We don't need plans for the technology; we need plans for learning outcomes. We need to consider how technology can broaden learning boundaries time, space, and relationships for each student.

For example, blogging is a wonderful resource teacher can use to increase student writing audiences and teach students how to manage their writing. A blog is a custom website where users can post anything they like: stories, reviews, images, multimedia presentations, etc. Blogs are fairly easy to configure, and content can be produced in minutes.

There's no doubt that when it comes to writing in school, being able to exchange thoughts with a wider audience changes the equation. Blogs encourage teachers to refocus their approach to writing instruction and show students how writing can be a very effective means of participating in connections and conversations. That is, the classroom can be a transformative motivator.

- **Staff Development:**

Yet a lot of teachers don't know much about podcasting to iPods, and they don't have time to learn. But some of the students there do. Instead of educating students, we could send them to an after-school workshop to learn how to podcast. See more articles explaining the students' potential to act as tech leaders.

For instructors, favorited questions are: What do you want to teach? Where is it that your students are fighting?

The teacher was worried the students might miss seeing the eggs hatch. They suggested setting up an incubator Webcam and a website that the video would be streaming to. The students were then able to make a slow-motion video about the whole process.

Tapping into what teachers want to do and aligning it is more effective with technology than helping teachers learn how to create PowerPoint presentations. Blogs constitute a classic example. They encourage better writing, a genuine audience, portfolio building, and self-reflection. But don't do a blogging workshop; offer a writing workshop and the authentic audience.

- **The Innovation Gap:**

Did you optimize your investment in your current technology? "The most popular response is," Not yet. "Several travels revealed two widening gaps: the gap in numbers (some students have more stuff) and the gap in the innovative application.

The winners are the students attending schools that use technology to lift standards of what all students should do. Two elements distinguish both schools: 24 x 7 learning opportunities and more rigor, discipline, and imagination in the design of student assignments.

- **Organizational Design:**

Program Directors that completely recognize networks' willingness to endorse and extend learning boundaries need to do so. This is why the network operator of the school system will answer directly to the Operator of the curriculum.

School systems will change network traffic to 24 x 7 learning from administrative tasks such as scheduling and payroll. The earlier we help the program leader transition from paper-based curricula to digital access, the better we can support students who aren't able to keep up in the classroom.

- **Plagiarism:**

Teachers may react by trying to catch the culprits or change assignments to make it almost impossible for the students to cheat.

When you delegate students to search the Internet for project sources, some can use the information without acquiring any real knowledge. The alternative is to offer academic challenges to the students who put little emphasis on cutting and pasting.

When students have a platform for their presentations, such as connecting a World History class with students using Skype in Japan, England, and Germany — or any video broadcasting system. They would be better prepared to discuss World War II lessons than if they were to give in a paper. And, the debate can be saved from the teacher's blog as an audio file for podcasting. This has a chilling impact on plagiarism as students know their research would be open to everyone to view.

- **Lack of Critical Thinking:**

Students who use the internet need to learn how to manage large quantities of knowledge, distinguish facts from fiction, think critically about the time spent on the web, and be secure. Being knowledge-literate ensures that a student understands Internet grammar: how to read a web address, recognize a website owner, and cross-reference knowledge to assess its legitimacy.

Too many schools use blocking sites to try to shield children. How frustrating it must be for a student using Google in a filtered school, and then using it in an unfiltered environment at home.

If we teach students what to do while they are alone, school filtering can be a cruel trick: "Now you're safe; now, you're not." Build guidelines for teaching students practical Internet thinking skills. We can't assume it will filter the rest of the world.

2.4 What's New In Google Classroom?

After its launch, the platform has been updated quite a bit, and Google continues to add new features, mostly based on teacher feedback frequently. For many years, users lament the lack of grading functionality or a tool for building rubrics in Google Classroom. Google has listened to and is launching a new method for gathering and marking works, called Assignments, late in the school year 2019-2020. Anyone with exposure to G Suite for Education should apply for a free preview of the beta assignments.

Google Classroom is a free software program. Google Classroom helps teachers and students connect and can be used to coordinate and handle tasks, to go paperless, to collaborate with students and teachers, to teach from afar, and so on! You may compare it to Showbie, as well as other online learning platforms or management systems.

It's on top of Google Docs and Google Drive, which means any instructor would find it very easy to use and intuitive. This doesn't mean it's dull, though. Google Classroom is full of new surprises that you'll come across along the way.

- Teachers and students must use accounts from the school and be in the same domain.
- Admins are expected to turn Google Meet on.
- Administrators can find more resources for distance learning at Setup Meet.

Things you can do with Google Classroom:

And the most relevant query is possibly this. How should you use the Classroom on Google? Who do you think is in it?

It's completely safe, first of all. You're not going to need to upgrade to a pro edition, which will save you more money. Hey, $0.00. None of that. At. Nothing.

You can get started after you have configured your classroom. Within just a few minutes, you'll find out how to set up your Google Classroom account. Let me first show you why Google Classroom's a big deal. Here's a rundown of what you should do about it:

- **Add Material:**

Send your students announcements about your class. The announcements include the lesson content. These announcements will appear in the Google Classroom stream of your students. That way, the students can easily find anything. You can attach materials from a Google drive, connect to that lesson in Google Classroom, add files and pictures from your phone, add a YouTube video, or add any other connection that your students want to see. That is so simple!

- **Add Assignments:**

Just like adding an announcement to your course, you can add an assignment. It operates the same way except you get the option of adding a due date and rating it here. When they have to make an assignment, it will alert the students, and it will also appear in their calendar.

- **Rate Assignment:**

Afterward, you may test and evaluate your student's assignments. There's space for input through a comment from an instructor. Then, return the task to your students. The

"Points" tab houses a grade book of the assignments and grades of the students.

- **Student Administrators:**

Of course, the students must be able to share their feedback. Or don't they? That is entirely up to you! You can handle permissions, allow students to post and comment, comment only, or grant the teacher the right to post and comment only. And the students can be e-mailed individually.

Things you can't do with Google Classroom:

Before you start using Google Classroom for the wrong reasons, there are a few things you should know. It's a forum for online learning, but it's not:

- **Chatbox:**

You may comment on assignments and notifications, but no talk feature is accessible. You can give them an email if you want to be in direct contact with your students, or you can allow other Google apps to take over this feature. Talk of Meet Hangouts.

- **A test or survey tool:**

There are several possibilities to do quizzes in Google School; however, it's not yet intended to be a survey tool alone. To that end, there are so many other useful features.

Choice 1: You can add assessments and assignments inside Google Classroom from other educational applications, such as an automatically graded Book Widgets test.

Choice 2: Inside Google Classroom itself, here's what you can do: add a question. Then select a clear answer or a question of multiple choices. We know, not this good. If you want to make a digital classroom more interactive, it's best to choose the first choice.

- **Discussion forum:**

You can make announcements, and students can vote on them, but it's not a great place to speak. Check out google if you're looking for a natural but powerful, free classroom resource that will inspire discussions (and other cool things).

Chapter 3: Starting With Google Classroom

The first thing you'll need to do when you open Google Classroom is to build a class. In the top-right corner, press the Plus button, and then pick the Build class. It will pop up a dialog box on the screen asking whether you intend to use Google Classroom for students at a school. If teachers plan to use it in their classes, Google Classroom allows schools to use G Suite for Education. That provides more privacy and security measures for teachers and students. When you use Google Classroom for your personal use, there's no need to think about that. If you want to create your class and getting started with google classroom, then read on. In this chapter, we explain to you how you can make your classroom.

3.1 Link Google Classroom

Google Classroom Linking Account allows you to connect to Realize with your Google Classroom account. Then you can synchronize students from your Google Classroom into Realize and share Realize assignments directly in feeds for students. If you've already logged in to Google Classroom but want to import additional Google Classroom classes, see Google Classes Sync.

You must sign in on your computer or mobile device to use the Classroom and then join classes. You can then get your teacher's work and communicate with your classmates. Upon joining a class on one device, you are enrolled on all devices in that class.

3.2 Explore Your Way through the Google Classroom

Google surely is no stranger to the educational market. The tech giant had high hopes when it debuted Google Classroom in 2014 that the tool will streamline daily classroom activities and give teachers more time to do what they do best.

We've seen the normal constraints applying to students and teachers in a classroom begin to fall away every day Around 10 million teachers and students had embraced it as part of their daily routines within a year after Google Classroom was released. Google Classroom has more than strengthened itself as a positive instance of classroom technology, with countless updates since.

Google Classroom Bolsters Collaborative Learning

The teachers can use Google Classroom to keep their paperwork organized in one dashboard for all their classes. With a few clicks, each class roster can be assigned homework digitally. Because of one simple thing, Google Classroom makes the jobs of educators easier: it eliminates trips to the copier.

Normally, if a teacher wants to build a worksheet for her students, she must create it in a word processor, make photocopies, print it out, hand it out to her students, hope that nobody loses it (which, of course, somebody always does) and then collect it when it's done. This process is streamlined for education with Google Classroom because teachers simply digitally create worksheets. Google has also made it easier to learn collaboratively.

Teachers can share data with their peers in one way — like a document that can be edited — and then share with students a different version — a document without editing functions. Discussions in the classroom are facilitated more easily by a student response system, which allows teachers to start question-driven discussions on the virtual page of their class. The Share Classroom extension with educators and send all their students a website or other content at once for a lesson.

The new extension allows me to engage my students and help them drive their learning on our school's 1:1 device.

Educator Prudence McKinney states that at Colony High School, Google Classroom is used "as a platform for students to access daily assignments. Provide students with faster, more detailed, and meaningful feedback and gives examples of educators giving out and grading a quiz in real-time, rather than waiting to return paper.

Using Google Classroom allows students to have instant feedback and gives the teacher a detailed item analysis on which questions the students answered correctly or incorrectly. At a glance, the teacher can view areas that may need to be re-teacher or clarified. Also, students who miss a class can easily catch up on assignments using a web-based classroom.

Google Classroom Advantages Ease Workflow for IT

Google Classroom is a good fit for IT teams and administrators. Alerts inform them of suspicious activity. IT teams can also control teachers, and students' password resets, so waiting time is minimal.

Using the application program interface (API), administrators and developers of new Ed-tech products can easily synchronize Google Classroom rosters with other platforms, such as a learning management system or an information system for students. API also enables teachers to use add-ons and other apps seamlessly within the Classroom environment.

With Google Classroom, administrators have access to all types of data. They can track trends in usage, active users, and classes as well as posts by students and teachers. With reports, as well as new ones to be added in the future, we hope that administrators will have the insights they have to provide their teachers and students with the best possible support.

Google Classroom Updates Stay in line with new Trends

Google has updated Classroom to current learning trends, including customization. A recent update makes it easy for teachers to create assignments for single students or groups. Google has claimed it as a discreet way of providing extra help to struggling students.

The use of Google Classroom in conjunction with Chrome books and G Suite for Education apps has enabled students to take responsibility for their learning, a key component of customization. In Maine Township High School District 207 in Illinois, Google Chat has helped foster a constant dialog between students and teachers. In a strictly pencil-and-paper world, teachers can give real-time feedback that's impossible.

Google tools and apps have created a collaborative environment that encourages even the youngest students to reach out to their teachers if they struggle. Second-graders at California's Arcadia Unified School District even send their teachers an email if they have homework problems. Google Classroom has expanded to include unique learning opportunities, such as post-school programs and adult learner workshops. Google also explored the use of Classroom to connect students through an international exchange program and found that the tool eliminated the intimidation factor.

3.3 Start Your First Google Class

Wouldn't it be excellent if you could organize your students' assignments, resources, and grades in a single location? Fortunately, Google listened to the teacher's needs attentively for EDU and designed Google Classroom to do just that. It's what we like to describe as the anti-LMS because it's both simple and effective. Students have a source of information for assignments, parents can see missing assignments and progress for the students, and educators can manage digital assignments and communication more easily.

Google Classroom makes teaching efficient and meaningful by providing educators with a hub for student assignments, boosting collaboration among students, and encouraging communication. Educators can create classes, distribute assignments, send feedback from individuals, and see everything in one place. The classroom also integrates seamlessly with other Google tools such as Calendar, Google Docs, Slides, Drive, and others. So if you want to start your classroom, then All right, we've got you so far. That means something Google Classroom needs to say to you. You will find it easy to set up and very intuitive to continue to use it. Follow those steps to set up your teacher account at Google Classroom:

Sign up:

When you go to googleclassroom.com, you may use Classroom through logging in with an e-mail address in the G folder, or you can use it for education without "claiming." That way, everything works just fine too. If you have hundreds of them, it's only easier to handle your pupils. You're going to have to add that one by one.

Create a Class

As a teacher, creating a class is one of the first things you'll do in the Classroom. In a class, students may be assigned work and post announcements. If you are teaching multiple classes (at the secondary level), then for each section you are teaching, you would create one class. I'll only have you creating one class for this exercise.

Follow the steps below to create your 1st class:

1. Go to the classroom.google.com. And sign in

2. Select Role

3 Teacher. Click the + symbol on the home page of Classroom, then select Create Class

4. Give the class a title that makes sense to you and your students

5. The following are optional but might be relevant to your situation of teaching:

- Click Section and enter the details to enter a short description of your class, grade level, or class time.
- Click Subject to add a subject such as Algebra I, and enter a name, or click one from the given list that appears when you enter text.
- Click Room to enter the classroom location, and enter the details.
- Click on the Create button.

You will now see a specific class code displayed, but that's not going to be necessary right now. When you are prepared to invite students to your class, we will come back to that at a later time. If you need to see the code at any time, you can view it on the Stream page.

Compliments! You now have your first Google Classroom created. You're well on your way to helping student learning by using Google Classroom. In the next chapter, before inviting the students, you will learn how to add assignments and resources to your class.

Invite students to your class:

Once you have built your class, you may invite your students to participate. Let them register by entering the unique code you've given them using the Google Classroom app. You can find the code in your class which was developed. Go to the "students" page. Another choice is to allow your students to enter their e-mail address, one by one. One thing you should bear in mind: your students need an e-mail address from Gmail or Google.

You can also visit classroom.google.com to let your students go. You can select "join class" there, enter the class code, and you are in! This might be a little easier because you don't have to type in the e-mail address of every student.

Now ready for your online class! At least, it's there, and it's open to everyone. You have to do a few other things before you can take off for good.

- Create an initial task or announce. You can share an announcement in the Path or go to Classwork-click on the "+ Build" button and send your first assignment to Google Classroom. Don't forget to have your tasks counted. The students will find it easier to see which one comes first because you can't reorder assignments in the stream. You can also transfer assignments up to the top. Click on the title to see if there are any students in the assignment, and to give grades and feedback. You should then return the tasks to your students so that they can start editing again.

- Add some lesson material to your class/task. Fill in Google Drive material or add a YouTube video, a computer file, a connection, etc. You will find those options right below the due date. If you just want to share your class presentation, which is not related to an assignment, you can go to the

"About" tab. A few lesson materials like slides, interesting articles, and examples can be added here.

- Open a tab on the Drive. Each time a new class is created, Google Classroom builds a Drive folder for that class. At any time, you can access the folder by going to all tiles in your class. You can find a folder icon on each piece of tile. Click on it in the folder you are. You can add resources for the class here too. Most of your student assignments end up in the Google Drive folder automatically, and you'll get it back whenever you want.

Chapter 4 Managing Your Google Classroom

The digital revolution in schools renders them completely paperless; teachers need to start seeking new approaches for handling their classroom, interacting with students, and handing out assignments. Google Classroom is a web service for classrooms, colleges, and educational institutions that have a personal Google Account; some of them find the right solution. Let's find out more about it.

4.1 Effectively Create Your Classroom Content

Proper lesson planning is essential to the learning and teaching process. A trained teacher is well on his / her way towards an excellent instructional experience. The production of interesting lessons requires a tremendous amount of time and energy. You must be committed, as a new teacher, to invest the requisite time in this Endeavor.

It is important to remember that the best-prepared lesson is useless if there is no proof of interesting execution procedures, along with effective management of the classroom techniques. A wide body of work is available relating to the creation and delivery of lessons and the importance of the management of classrooms. They are skills that need to be researched, tailored to your specific style, applied in a teacher/learning environment, and reviewed and constantly updated as needed. Consistency is of the utmost importance when developing a management program for classrooms.

All the teachers will understand that they are not an island. The district's educational philosophy and the individuality of their schools will be the key to what's happening in the classroom. The code of discipline of the school, which should be fair, responsible, and meaningful, has to be expressed in the classroom management efforts of every teacher.

Students of all ages continue to learn by creating – it helps to synthesize knowledge and introduce fun and sense into their educational experience. There are a few main steps that teachers can take to build a more inventive, accessible, creative, and trustworthy environment for students to develop, take risks, and feel confident with their learning patterns.

1. Address Student Needs:

Recall that students, like adults, have not only physical needs but also important psychological requirements for security and order, love and belonging, personal ambition and competence, freedom and novelty, and fun. Students are continually motivated to satisfy all those needs, not just two or three of them. As teachers actively discuss these needs in the classroom, students are happy to be there, instances of aggression arise far less often, and student involvement and learning.

2. Build a Sense of Order:

Both students need a framework and want to know that their instructor not only understands his field of content but also knows how to handle his classroom. The teacher has to offer specific behavioral and academic expectations right from the start — students should always know what is expected of them. Another essential way to establish a sense of order is by introducing appropriate procedures to the students for the various realistic activities performed in the classroom. For example, teach students how to:

- Reach the classroom and get interested in a learning activity immediately
- Distribute and gather materials

- Find out about missing assignments due to absence and how to make them up
- Get the attention of the instructor without disrupting the class
- Arrange their desks quickly and respectfully for various purposes: in front rows for direct instruction.

3. Greet Students Every Day

When students enter your classroom, greet every student at the entrance. Explain why you want students to make eye contact with you, give you a verbal greeting, and - depending on the students' age - a five-high, fist bump, or handshake. Every student has had meaningful human interaction this way, at least once that day. It also shows the students that as people, you care for them. If a student was disruptive or uncooperative the day before, it gives you a chance to check-in, clarify your theory of "every day is a clean slate," and demonstrate hope for that class ("Let's have a great day now").

4. Get to know your students:

The more you know about the backgrounds, interests, extracurricular activities, personalities, learning styles, aspirations, and mindsets of your students, the more you will be able to understand them and teach them. Anyways to get to know your students:

- Inform yourself about their cultures
- Speak to them
- Give journal questions and read and address them
- Attend extracurricular activities
- Have students complete interest inventories or surveys

- Have students' complete learning style and personality tests
- Have daily class meetings
- Play team-building games with students.

5. Avoid Rewarding to Control:

Over 50 years of studies have shown that bonuses, gold stars, awards, monetary rewards, A's, and other bribes only serve to weaken the inherent motivation of students, build relationship issues and lead students to do nothing without a guaranteed reward. The human brain does have its scheme of rewards. If students excel in a difficult task, whether it be academic (a presentation of a class) or behavioral (going through a class without blurring out), their brains get a shot of endorphins. Instead of using stickers or badges to devalue their achievements, speak to students about how it feels to gain the ability and appreciate the initiative, techniques, and processes that led them to those achievements. Then explore what they've learned this time to help them reach their next successes.

6. Avoid Judging:

When students feel they are being criticized, pigeonholed, and branded, they mistrust the judging individual. It is hard not to criticize a student who is just sitting there doing no schoolwork after having done everything you can to inspire her. It's easy to see how we could find these lazy graduates. And it's easy to mark the student as a bully, who constantly provokes and threatens peers. But punishing and marking students is not just a way to shirk our duty of educating them ("There's nothing I can do about Jonny. He's incorrigible."). Still, it also ignores the underlying question entirely. Be interested, rather than judging the students. Only question why. (Where does this fear or aggression come from?) Once you discover the underlying cause for the actions, this problem can be approached directly, eliminating all the time and energy it consumes for the students to cajole, coerce, and offer consequences.

7. Employ Class-Building Games and Activities:

Developing positive relationships with your students is essential; developing positive relationships among them is equally important. Engaging students in non-competitive games and cooperative learning mechanisms is one of the best ways to break down the cliques inside a classroom and help shy or new students feel a sense of belonging. Online and in books, there are hundreds of resources that provide thousands of suitable choices for your grade level. Another advantage of getting play in the classroom is that it offers a powerful incentive for your students to come to your class — it's fun.

8. Be Vulnerable:

Becoming vulnerable builds trust more rapidly than any other method. Recognizing your mistakes shows you are human and makes you more available. This also sends the message in this classroom that it is okay to make mistakes. And we're thinking. Vulnerability and public self-assessment often help to build a culture of growth mentality: we tolerate mistakes rather than at all costs seeking to prevent them. We learn and grow from those mistakes. Make a little mistake, like spilling a glass of water or misspelling a word on the board, and talk about how you're glad you made a mistake because it taught you something, instead of making excuses.

9. Celebrate Success

At first, this growth seems to contradict incentives avoiding strategy six. It isn't. A celebration is a spontaneous occurrence organized to celebrate an accomplishment. As an "if-you-do-this-then-you-get-that" incentive, it is not hinted at or confirmed before time. Alternatively, you could set a class target, like the entire class achieving 80 percent or higher on an assessment. Label the progress of students on a wall map (percentages, not individual names). Discuss the methods, procedures, or study habits that students used to be productive with each assessment, and what they learned and should do to build upon the next assessment. Host a celebration until the class is attaining the target. It should not be a circus of three rings. It would be enough to show some amusing or interesting (appropriate) online videos, to carry in cupcakes, or to play some non-competitive games. The next time you set a target for a class, and the students ask if you're going to celebrate again, do not automatically tell them. It is not just about cupcakes; it is about work and learning.

10. Mindset:

A shift in attitude, mood, and the overall atmosphere of the classroom starts with the teacher. The teacher sets the class tone from the minute that students step into the classroom. If educators are passionate about their subject matter, they continue to obey the students. Educators must be enthusiastic about the subjects which they teach. Nevertheless, the attitude of an instructor about how to develop and produce content is key to the creative process of learning. Most teachers were qualified to educate solely from the instructor. To shift this kind of delivery and make the classroom more creative, they need to think of their students as leaders too — acting as guides instead of teaching material and asking students to spill out knowledge on a standardized test.

11. Self-reflection:

Self-reflection in the classroom is for teachers to look back on their teaching methods and figure out how and why they were teaching and how their students reacted in a certain way.

For a career as daunting as teaching, self-reflection will provide teachers with a vital opportunity to see what succeeded in their classroom, and what failed. To order to concentrate on what works, educators should use reflective instruction as a way to assess and evaluate their teaching practices. Good teachers accept the fact that there is always scope for change in teaching methods, implementation, and performance.

12. Ask Open-Ended Questions:

Open-ended questions are questions that are not addressed throughout a textbook. As educators ask open-ended questions, there may be multiple answers and perspectives. Student responses can lead to good cooperation, stimulating discussions, new ideas, and the development of leadership skills. This exercise may also help students understand the potential they have never found inside. They may also make comparisons to their own lives through open-ended questions, inside other stories, or to real-world events.

13. Build Versatile Learning Environments:

With different teaching strategies, teachers need to think about how to use their classroom space. For example, when teachers can quickly shift furniture around the room, they can find it is a crucial variable for enhancing learning for students. Because teaching has changed, the classroom space needs to provide students with opportunities to work independently, connect with their peers, and provide collaborative areas. Most of today's classrooms are still crowded, cluttered, noisy spaces that lack the space to move about with ease, create communication gaps, and lead to roadblocks when students need to concentrate.

There should be flexible working spaces and versatility to encourage one-to-one working, teamwork, critical thought, and community discussions.

14. Personality Matters: Build A Position For All Learners

The Influence of Introverts in a World That Can't Stop Talking, one of the crucial distinctions between extroverts and introverts, extroverts prefer more to get their energy from social contact, and introverts to obtain power from quiet spaces and a time to think and focus alone.

Therefore, when a classroom is based solely on group work — which emphasizes entire group discussions, small groups working together, gathering peer input (all of which require a lot of social interaction), and extroverts in the classroom will develop and gain energy. At the same time, introverted students will quickly find themselves exhausted with a lack of motivation to take part.

Also, the reverse is likely to happen when a project focuses solely on quiet contemplation or individual study. Introverts will then blossom and flourish, causing extroverts to feel antsy and confused. Also, they can quickly get irritated or have trouble trying to get attention, chat, creep in on social media, and get disruptive.

Teachers should provide opportunities for students to work in groups or on their own, where possible. Extroverts can complete specific tasks on their own, and introverts can choose to work together—both of these ways of teaching are crucial to fulfilling specific learners' needs.

Teachers who have opportunities that better involve, encourage, and retain the enjoyment of learning for students are likely to put in their best efforts, appreciate the process, and achieve positive results.

15. Using Problem-Finding:

Instead of problem-solving, teachers may help students look at the world through using problem-finding to identify holes to fill in. Seeking problems is equivalent to finding problems.

Teachers should use problem-finding as part of a broader problem-finding method as a whole, which should involve problem-forming and problem-solving all together. Problem-finding requires an analytical and creative imagination to figure out what might be lacking or something important that should be added to it. Teachers should use this technique to give students the ability to think deeply, ask hard questions, and find innovative ways to solve problems.

16. Let Students Take Chances And Fail:

Students have to understand that adults attempt a lot of things throughout their lives and frequently struggle yet keep trying. Students need to undergo a learning loss.

When teachers have real-world projects that can solve problems for students, they allow students to learn from failure, move up again and again, and finally achieve success. If we don't let the students fail, we are most certainly not only holding back the growth of individual students but also holding back the entire education system.

We're teaching students that their experiences matter by giving them real-world challenges to solve, struggle, and try again. We have plenty of things worth dealing with, which we can provide students with feedback and opinion.

A discovery and inquiry-based pedagogy are so much more exciting than remembering the dates, facts, and testing. Pre-determined answers to an exam in a conventional setting in education will hold back the students in ways that we cannot test.

17. Imagine A Flipped Classroom Model:

If teachers using a flipped model throughout the classroom, the conventional sequence of teaching and classroom activities is set back. Students may usually display lecture materials, read the text, or do study as their homework before entering college. The time spent in class is for tasks that could include peer-to-peer learning, group discussions, independent learning, and participating in discussions or collaborative research. And 71 percent of teachers who flipped their classes recorded an increase in grades, according to the Learning Network, while 80 percent reported better student attitudes as a result. Also, the following year, 99 percent of teachers who flipped their classes said they would flip their classes again.

18. Welcome Pioneers And Innovators Into The Classroom:

Utilizing technology as a place to interact and touch, teachers may welcome entrepreneurs in different ways to their classrooms. With one click of a button, educators can reach out to varying leaders via social media platforms such as LinkedIn or Twitter. Invite these leaders into the classroom either through live contact or by interactive means such as Skype. Teachers may just be shocked how many innovative innovators are looking to give back — and giving back to youth can be rewarding ways to make a difference for a good founder. For starters, if you follow online class, you will see a host of innovators and entrepreneurs who has been involved with his classes and continue to be involved. What is the worst thing that can happen with a request? Not too much.

19. Using the design-thinking method:

The design-thinking method is a collection of organized techniques that recognize problems, collect knowledge, generate possible solutions, develop ideas, and test solutions.

The cycle has five phases: exploration, understanding, thinking, experimentation, and evolution.

Students and teachers can follow this pattern for each phase:

- I've got a challenge. How do I get at it?
- I have learned everything. How do I perceive it now?
- I see the chance. What should I do?
- I just got an idea. How can I make this?
- I tried something different, something different. Why do I make that evolve?

Both these methods are ways in which innovation can be shaped and imagination motivated in education. Teachers should start with a new project and see how things go with their students while constantly evaluating learning and building. Innovation is a crucial change that we need today in schools, and that can start with you.

4.2 Adding an Assignment and grading it

If you have your Google Classroom's basic framework in place, you can start assigning the work to your students. BEFORE that you are assigning tasks, consider the system you would like to use to coordinate all assignments. Until making tasks, you need to figure out the structure. Unable to switch assignments after confirmation.

Create Topics Or Categories:

After making a task, but AFTER assigning it, go to the menu on the right hand. Having a subject has drop-down. It is still there after you have produced a subject. Which topics will you be creating? This belongs to you! Consider developing topics by subject, by year, or weekday. Whatever makes more sense to you as the instructor organizationally and is quick to connect with your students would be the best.

Posting Assignments:

Just post assignments if you want students to work on them. Even, you can make assignments and save them as drafts. When you post an assignment, it goes public and finalizes it for your students.

Make assignments in advance, on that note. You can batch them, and you can make more. Only keep them in draft form and allocate them when you want students to work on them.

One idea is to number tasks if you want the students in a particular order to complete them. It lets students know the order in which they were posted and the order you intend to complete them in.

Arrange Posts:

You may arrange a mailing. That will help you batch and allocate your work over a while. Would you like students to one day read a passage and address questions that day? Establish them two different tasks and schedule them separately.

Hide Notifications In Your Stream:

Hiding alerts in YOUR stream makes things simpler and stops all the tasks you allocate to the classwork from showing up. This keeps the stream engaged in announcements rather than all the updates.

Build Several Classrooms:

Instead of creating specific topics above (which you can do apart from this suggestion), consider creating particular classrooms. You could have a classroom for math and a classroom for language arts. Post each assignment and group the topics by date inside the classroom.

Have A Category For "Other Fun Stuff"?

This can take place where you post links and files that students can do if they choose to delve deeper into a subject or website. This is a position where parents who are seeking further tasks can also post extra work.

Assigning work to the students

Here are some times how you can assign work to the students

Create a copy of your file.

Hold the initial document to remove slides from the edition you are assigning to the students. So you only need to send them one graphic organizer at the time but have ALL of the graphic organizers in one main text. This best practice extends to all of the services that you have at Google. Create copies of your original, so your students don't screw up.

Show the copies in folders

View The COPY in a folder for all originals. Shift the STUDENT COPY into a folder that the students are assigned to. This keeps your originals and student copies apart, and places all the student files in one place, making them readily available when posting assignments.

Adjust the settings of the share

To get students to type in the text, you need to offer the students EDIT access.

Grade an Assignment

You can enter grades in the Assignments grading tool, along with your teaching assistants. Every grader requires an Education account with a G Suite.

After returning a work, work file ownership transfers back to the student. Then, students can see their reviews and ratings.

The default denominator for the degree is 100. You can alter it to any number which is greater than zero. You can also change the grade denominator at any time, but only unreturned assignments are affected by that adjustment. Assignments returned except their original denominator.

Without a mark, you will return one task. If you use Assignments LTI, however, the LMS cannot differentiate between ungraded assignments and unsubmitted assignments.

Follow the steps in your Assignment edition.

If you are using Assignments next to an LMS:

1. Go to classroom.google.com.
2. Click Caption.

3. Click the submission of the student.
4. Join the grade below Degree. Your score as a draft save.
5. To grade another task, press the Down arrow next to the name of the subject and select another subject.

When using Assignments LTI in an LMS:
1. Go to the LMS.
2. Click on Attribution Open in Assignments.
3. Click the submission of the student.
4. Join the grade below Degree. Your score as a draft save.
5. To grade another task, press the Down arrow next to the name of the subject and select another course.

Return assignment:

If an assignment is returned, control of the assignment file is transferred back to the student. Students may have their thoughts and feedback presented.

A copy of the task returned is saved to your Google Drive. You also have a copy of the graded assignment to use as proof of plagiarism in case a student disputes their degree, for accreditation purposes, or even if the student changes the original assignment, or deletes it, the assignment copy is secure.

The student receives an email that notifies them about ranking the task. The email has a link to see the Assignments graded work. The student can see the ranking, remarks on the margins, and general feedback.

When the student receives the graded assignment, they may either respond to feedback from individual margins or review and resubmit their paper. The student may begin discussions or conclude comments. Initial comments from the professor transfer the returned assignment to their copy

Notify students of the returned classwork:

When returning student assignment data, assignments, and assignments, LTI will automatically contact the student. The email directly links to the assignment page where students can view files submitted, feedback on the overall task, and ranking.

While any assignment or quiz you submit to your Community can be added to the Gradebook automatically, we do not know that all assignments will be posted using Edmodo.

Do the following to add grades for Assignments or Quizzes not posted by Edmodo:

- Click the "Add Grade" button in the top right corner of the Grade Book.
- Include the task title and the total number of potential points for the task.
- Press the "Create" button.

A new grade column will be created-it will be blank because Edmodo doesn't generate results. You can manually add grades by clicking on the student's blank grade area and typing into the grade.

4.3 Sharing Resources and Links

In technology, class relations are like digital currencies. If you're in the right places with the right ones, you can easily open doors to excellent learning opportunities.

The goal is to have them at the right time and to be able to deliver to the students. Teachers often ask me, "That's a wonderful activity, and I would love to do it, but how do my students access it? "And they say," What do the students do after they've done it to me? "Resources and Resource Collections also provide a 'Share' option that permits to be shared with other users, also with non-users of the program, to make usage more versatile.

The resource itself is never sent directly to users or non-users. Instead, a URL is created to act as a connection to the resources. Allowing for easy and safe sharing even of large collections. The links contain a unique key that only allows access to that specific resource or set, and the sender can choose the level of access the recipient will have.

Email:

After clicking on this option, you can enter a list of user names in Resource Space (you can also enter full names or groups) or external email addresses to submit a resource or set connection. The user will provide an internal access link to the resource/collection, and an external access link will be given to a non-user (external email address). You will be required to have an External Access to Assets permit standard and expiry date. Also, to make them more personalized, you can add a message to your inbox.

Generate URL:

You can either create an internal connection that can be sent to other device users or an external connection that can be used by anyone to view the resources. You can then copy and give them the link as necessary so that they can access the resource or set.

When creating an external share, you can set:

- Access level / Share expiry date
- The user group that the external user emulates

- A password to access the share (optional)

Modifying or deleting an external share password

Once an external share password has been set, it cannot be displayed but can be modified or deleted.

To do so, follow the steps to share the collection or resource as previously, and you will see a list of registered external shares. Click on the corresponding share Id or edit link. You can either type a new password (or delete it entirely from the password field) before clicking Save

Sharing via social media:

Resources and collections can be shared on social media channels using the icons given under the column 'Social media.' At the moment, links to Resource Space can be shared through Facebook, Twitter, and LinkedIn.

These links can be cached by modifying the value of $social media links contained in config.default.php

4.4 Keep Google Feeds Clean

On the Android phone, the Google Feed (formerly known as Google Now) feature is considered fantastic by some users and irritating by others. Some users rely on their Google Feed cards, while others find them distracting and frustrating. Here's how to turn on or off that app.

1. Click "Download" from the Home screen.
2. Pick "Google"
3. Press the upper-left corner of the "Menu" button.
4. Pick "Configuration"
5. Choose "Your feed."

6. Set your settings as desired on the computer

- The configuration of "Notifications" determines whether changes are reflected in the notification area or not. Set it as needed, to "On" or "Off." You can set a choice for Ringtone or Vibrate on urgent updates, too.

- The "Feed" setting switches on and off the entire Google Now app. You can also uninstall your Google Feed preferences when picked, and disable Google Feed on all devices linked to your account.

4.5 Student Performance Management Tips

Teachers need to get to know EVERY student. Students who earn good grades cannot simply improve their academic skills by performing well on exams. Some of them have to write better if they want to be successful at college. Others need to know how to communicate with their classmates properly. Others need to be inspired to turn themselves from students who do well on exams into students who can start and ends independent projects — the kind of skill they need to excel in college and the workplace.

And then the shy graduates. Many of them were in grammar and high school schools. They lacked the belief that they should talk in class, so they did not. Their grades were good to outstanding, but for them to offer their thoughts and observations, they needed someone to spur them. Their oral communication skills had to be developed.

You had to end the presumption that teachers and administrators will concentrate their attention on the students with problems. In particular, teachers will go out of their way for each student to spend about the same time. Lisa Simpson merits the same recognition that Bart Simpson deserves.

The advice a teacher gives to a student should be private. While the most important thing that teachers can do is emphasize the good about the success of a student. Telling her or him three things she or he did right before going into constructive feedback — it is also important that other students don't hear the criticisms.

In short, teachers need to communicate privately on one with the student than for employers to communicate privately on one with the employee. It is more important for students at all grade levels, but for high school students, it is more important than for grammar school students.

Before we get into the step-by-step part of what a teacher has to do to formulate an effective communication strategy with students, we want to stress how important it is to have a positive frame of mind before starting. As a teacher, when running a classroom of 20 or 30 students, you can be disciplinary, but in one-on-one sessions, you should not be disciplinary. It's important to emphasize the positive.

If you are reviewing an assignment for fictional writing, you may praise the creativity, dialog, and characters of the author. You should get into the vulnerabilities, THEN. Many people have told us they hate writing because a teacher underlined their mistakes in spelling and grammar. Stressing the negative can prevent students from developing a significant skill.

Before the school year starts, you will have a schedule for private one-on-one interaction with your students. That means planning out the amount of time you expect to spend with students. We recommend a 10-minute meeting with every student once a month. The meeting's logistics could be determined by your classroom setting. You want to be mindful of the time students spend during class, so private meetings when the majority of the students are working on an assignment is a choice.

Inform the students about your plans to meet them one on one on the first day of class. Know, a lot of students are conditioned to face a teacher only when they have done something wrong. Put your proposal on a separate sheet of paper from the course syllabus in writing, and the rules of your classroom (which students will help draft). Emphasize in your plan that your goal is to collaborate with each student to develop their academic skills. It should mention skills such as critical thinking, the ability to ask, compose, and speak.

It's probably important to tell administrators about your plans, but it's also essential to inform parents of your students. Urge the students to submit all the written material you gave them on the first day of class to their parents. If you have one or find out a way to connect with parents, post your plans on your class website or class Facebook page. It is important to keep the parents updated about the success of their children. Emphasize for Any student you meet.

Communicating with parents may help you avoid the issue of one-on-one classroom meetings where your classmates can hear the conversation. Privacy is important if meetings are to be successful. Ask parents if post-school meetings are appropriate if you are unable to meet students privately in your classroom or neighboring space, and track other students simultaneously. Post-school meetings are insensitive, without the consent of parents and students. Meetings during study halls can also be held in your office.

Do not waste more time in your formal one-on-one meetings with some students than others — and remind the students that this is your preference. Students will easily infer that if you spend more time with any of them, you have favorites. You should also make yourself accessible to students who are needing assistance outside the one-on-one meeting setting but make it 100% clear that you are supporting all of your students to try this kind of support.

Some students respond to constructive feedback extremely well, but others do not. During the school year, you'll learn which kid gloves will be used to handle students. Finding input from parents of these students is an ideal way to learn how to give them guidance and suggestions. Watch the expressions of the students as you speak to them so that you know when to praise them for increasing their morale.

In your first meeting, emphasize that you have high standards for EVERY student. Students with poor or worse grades can have low standards because they have had years of difficulty at school. It is YOUR responsibility to improve their morale and remind them that each student has skills that will help them excel in life even if the student is unaware of those skills or their abilities have not improved their grades. Tell the students that you're going to work with them to discover and develop those skills. Be sure that during the school year, you must insist on the high standards.

Many students — and adults — for some unknown reason find making notes as a sign that your memory is deficient. The students already know the notes are being made. Tell them why and invite them to take notes, too. Emphasize that they can receive very detailed guidance and suggestions, and they can write down the highlights and review their notes as they try to develop their skills.

These meetings aim to support each student. Some students can change more over the school year than others. It's necessary to evaluate the progress of each person but be precise without making a judgment. Hopefully, your guidance and suggestions will enhance the performance of the students on exams and class assignments, but they are a different concern from your one-on-one discussions.

Even if you want your students to show who they are so that you can help them learn, they do NOT work both ways. They can tell you about their lives, but you shouldn't be reciprocating. It is necessary to relate stories from your life as a teacher and as a student that could help them understand. You can tell them, for example, that writing to public figures as a child has sparked your interest in social studies. Nevertheless, it is not acceptable to inform them about personal problems unrelated to their learning and to get together as friends outside of college.

This tip seems simple, but it's worth noting. Some students may disagree with your interpretation and your advice and suggestions on their work. Arguing with them is at best counter-productive, disrespectful, and, at worst, unprofessional. It is important to focus on what to say to those students who disagree with you. You might say something like, "I appreciate your views. You may as well be right. My opinion is, therefore, focused on ten years of teaching and working with hundreds of students. That doesn't mean I'm right, but I think it's true for my view. "Students and adults don't like someone who behaves like a know-it-all. Teachers who judge others are particularly vulnerable to criticism if they are behaving like they never make mistakes. If you have made a mistake, like offering advice that doesn't work, admit it. The students would like you more and have more faith in you. Trust is necessary if they will, in the future, listen to you. Additionally, students always know when the teacher made an error.

Providing comprehensive guidance to students is important, but the overall review of their work should be streamlined.

Once every session, you will sum up their results. Don't mention more than 5 or 6 competencies. What skills you mention depends on the topic you teach. Still, examples of skills work well with students, writing, speaking, problem-solving, creative thinking, critical thinking, analysis, reading comprehension, and completing assignments. Using the same categories during the school year promotes students' ability to track their progress.

You just told a student that in her essay, she did three things right — it was well-organized, written in a reader-friendly way, and had findings that were backed by the facts cited in the essay. Now, you give her constructive advice — she needs improvement in her spelling and grammar. Don't circle every mistake. That saps morale for a student. Offer her advice to build on the HOW instead. You might send her a book called "Guide to Grammar." Or you could tell her to read a certain number of books or periodicals, or some sort of book or newspaper. Be concrete.

Do NOT teach when arriving at constructive criticism. Rather than the equivalent of an employer assessing an employee's results, you should treat this meeting as a discussion. Encourage students to ask appraisal questions. In a one-on-one meeting, you want to express a few important points but don't try to dominate the meeting. Note the value of listening!!

Many students do not comprehend this zealous attempt to develop their skills. They think that their skills are great, particularly when they are getting good grades. You have to emphasize what they might need.

4.6 Encourage Collaboration between Students

Teamwork is a key skill students will learn at an early age. Students who collaborate with others can develop awareness and learn how to solve common problems. But creating teamwork between students in the classroom can often be a challenge, so teachers must promote it.

- **Incentives:**

Often all students need is a little bit of a motivation to collaborate with others. The drive can be a reward in the form of extra credit or unique stickers, which at the end of the course, students can redeem for prizes. Having teamwork a mandatory part of the curriculum in the classroom will make the students work together better. Introverted students are often motivated by teamwork to break out of their shell and become confident in collaborating with others.

- **Cooperation activities:**

A sports team is one illustration of coordination. The team consists of a group of people who work together to share knowledge of the game and their opponent to achieve a common objective. There is no choice why you can't provide the same type of environment in the classroom. An instructor will begin by integrating competitive teamwork exercises into the course programs and separating the class into teams, tasking them with the basic goal of beating the others. It can be a fun way to make the students feel more relaxed and collaborative.

- **Set a tone:**

-the class has the one disruptive student who speaks out and often makes classmates feel dumb or awkward and less likely to work on group projects. Early in the school year, teachers will set a standard and let it be known that disruptive conduct is inappropriate at any time. Make sure students understand that the class is a supportive, caring, and healthy environment;

this will allow them to engage and work together more effectively.

- **Group projects:**

Many students loathe group projects, but at the same time, there might be no activity that promotes more excellent teamwork than such types of tasks. The concept behind group projects is to inspire students to prepare and collaborate with others whether to meet after school in the library or at one of the households of group members. Make sure that every student in the community has a different position in contributing to the result.

- **Partners with parents:**

Teachers can take advantage of open houses and parent-teacher conferences to speak to their parents regarding issues such as student engagement. Letting parents know how essential teamwork is in the classroom can be an additional driving factor in motivating students to work together.

Chapter 5: Basics of Google Classroom for Students

The classroom is designed to help teachers build and collect paperless assignments with time-saving features such as the ability for each student to make a copy of a Google document automatically. It also generates Drive files for each task, which helps to keep everyone coordinated for each project. Students can continue track of what's due on the Assignments page and start working just one click away. Teachers will quickly see who completed the work or who didn't and provide clear, real-time feedback and grades right in the Classroom. Google Classroom also helps students in many ways, to know more about the basics keep reading!

5.1 Students' Managing Classes

- **Join a class**

You must sign in on your computer or mobile device to use the Classroom, and then attend classes. You will then get your teacher's work and interact with your classmates. Upon entering a class on one device, you are enrolled on all devices in that class.

How to join a class

You have 2 ways to enter a google class:

Join a class code

If your teacher gives you a class code, use this code to add yourself to the class. Your teacher may provide you the code while you're in the classroom, or email it.

Accept your teacher's invitation.

If your teacher sends you an invitation, you will see Join on your Classroom homepage on your class card.

Did the class code go forgotten or lost? Won't code work?

If you have deleted, lost, or forgotten your class code before you join a class, ask your teacher to resend the code. If the code doesn't work, ask your professor for help.

Note: To join the class, you will only use the class code once. You are easily then enrolled in the class and need not re-use the code.

Join a class

Sign in to the Classroom before you can join a class. Uncertain if you have signed in? Learn more about how to sign up for the Classroom.

Join a class with a code

1. Go to the classroom.google.com.
2. Make sure you sign in with the proper account. If you are already signed in and need to switch accounts, click in the top-right corner to select your profile image or add your account.
3. Click Add Class Join at the top.
4. Enter your teacher's class code, and then click Join.

A class code is composed of 6 letters or 7 numbers. Hjhmgrk, or g5gdp1, for example.

Accept your teacher's invitation.

1. Go to the classroom.google.com.
2. Make sure you sign in with the proper account. If you are already signed in and need to switch accounts, click in the top-right corner to select your profile image or add your account.

3. Click Join on the Class card.

- **Un-enroll from a class**

You can no longer see it in the Classroom when you unenrolled from a class, but all your class files will be saved in your Google Drive.

If you have mistakenly de-registered from a class and need to re-register, see Enter a class as a student.

Note: from Android iPhone & iPad machine, you cannot unregister from an existing class. Contact your instructor, and ask them to unachieved the class to unregister.

1. Go to the classroom.google.com.
2. Select the Classes tab.
3. Press Unenrolled for more on the lesson.
4. Press Unenrolled to confirm.

- **View an archived class**

Your teacher could archive it once a class ends. You are archiving extracts the class from your Classroom homepage and positions it in a separate area, which makes it easier to manage your website.

Even teachers can record a lesson or delete it. If you want to delete a class from your homepage, Unenrolled from a class should be needed.

Note: You are not allowed to unregister from an archived class.

When archiving a class:

1. It's deleted from your homepage.
2. You can see their materials, but you can't apply for any work.

116

3. Google Drive class folder also helps you to access class materials.

4. You cannot unsubscribe from this. Tell your instructor if you need to unenroll from an archived class.

Android iPhone & iPad computers

1. Go to the classroom.google.com.

3. Click Menu at the end.

3. Tap Archived Classes and scroll down.

4. Tap on the class you wish to see.

Note: If you have not saved any of your courses, this option does not appear on the menu.

- **View your class resource page**

Also, teachers in the Classroom can build video-meetings. All video meetings produced in the Classroom are called nicknamed meetings because if the teacher is the last person to quit, students cannot start a meeting before the teacher, or enter the meeting. Such permissions will vary according to how the school administrator sets up Meet.

Meet in the Classroom:

1. Teachers and students use school accounts and are on the same domain to use

2. Admins are expected to turn Google Meet on.

3. Admins will find more help for distance learning at Setting up Meet.

Furthermore, the premium G Suite Enterprise for Education apps will be available free of charge to all Classroom educators using G Suite for Education by September 30th, 2020. Such apps include live streaming, recording, and video meetings for class 250 students. Video meetings are available on the Classroom's Web and Smartphone versions.

5.2 Managing Assignments

You have many ways to view your work for a class:
1. See the upcoming work on the Classes page easily
2. See your work for a class on the work page
3. Search work by class on the To-do page
4. See the current work on the Stream page
5. See the work grouped by subject on the Classwork page

Quickly see upcoming work:

You will see work due within a week on the Classes tab, on a Class List. You'll see up to 3 things in the description and due date.
1. Go to the classroom.google.com.
2. (Optional) Click on the working title to view information.

See your work for a class on the work page:

A list of all your work can be seen on the Your Work tab. You will review your grades, review assignments, and due dates and see any late or missed work. You may also filter your work by status: Given, Grade Returned, or Skipped. You may display additional information, such as comments or attachments if you wish.
1. went to **classroom.google.com**.
2. Choose the option:
- On a class card, click on your work.

- Click on the class-------**Classwork**-----------**View your work.**

    3. (Optional) Click the title of the work View Information to see attachments, notes, or additional information for an assignment or query.

    4. (Optional) Click Assigned, Returned with Rank, or missing to filter your work, under Filters.

Filter your classwork

You can filter work by class on the To-do tab, and display work that is:

- To-do — Work assigned and not yet completed. You will see the names of class and work listed as missing, no due date, due today, or during the week, or afterward.

- Done — Work you've done, and turned in. When the work is classified, you'll see the work status — turned in or finished late — and gradations.

See the current work on the Stream page.

The latest research and updates can be seen on the Stream tab. The new post is still up at the end.

    1. Go to the classrrom.google.com.
    2. Click on the link.
    3. (Optional) Click on the task of the query to see any guidance or feedback.

See the work grouped by subject on the Classwork page

Your instructor can organize work by subjects on the Classwork page, such as homework or essays.

    1. Go to the classroom.google.com.

2. Click on the link.
3. Click on Classwork, at the end.
4. Look for a question or assignment under a subject.
5. (Optional) to show any directions or suggestions, click on Assignment show or Question view link.

- **Submit an assignment**

You can send in a personal doc that your instructor has given to you, create your own Google Doc, or add new files to the assignment, depending on the assignment.

You that resubmit the assignment if you need to edit the work that you have turned in. But any assignment completed after the due date turned in or marked is reported as late.

1. Go to the classroom.google.com.
2. Tap the class———Classwork—— class assignment
3. Attaching an object to:
   - Click Add or build under your work —- Select Google Drive, Connect, or File.
   - Pick the attachment for a connection or enter the URL, and press Connect.

Note: You are not allowed to add a file you do not own.4. for attaching a new doc;

Click Add, or create Files, Slides, Cards, or Sketches under Your work.

- A new file connects and opens to your work.
- Click on the file and enter your data.
- Note: You can add more than one file, or build it.

4. (Optional) to delete an attachment, press Delete. Next to the attachment name.

5. (Optional) Under Private Comments, add a private message to your instructor, enter your message and press Mail.
6. Click Turn In and verify.

Label an assignment completed.

Any work that is turned in or marked after the due date is reported as late, even though you submitted the work before the due date before.

1. Go to the classroom.google.com.
2. Click Task class Classwork.
3. (Optional) add a private message for your instructor under Private Comments and press Mail.
4. Select Confirm and Mark as done.
5. The attribution status changes to Handed in.

Check for late or missed assignments.

The instructor establishes the class' late work policies. The classroom isn't stopping you from handing in late work, however.

When assigning work to your instructor, it is labeled Assigned. Whether you don't hand in your work on time, Late or Completed would be reported late as the due date or time comes in. When research is due at 9:00 AM, for example, hand it in at 8:59 AM. This is late when you hand it in at 9:00 AM.

1. Go to the classroom.google.com.

2. Click your work on a class file.

3. To the right, you see each item's work status:

- Assigned — Job assigned by your instructor. Test your due date.
- Turn in — Work you came in on time.
- Graded — you see your score for graduated research that your instructor has returned.

- Returned — you see a check for ungraded work returned by your instructor.
- Missing — you didn't sign up to work.
- Hand in: Done late — Work you did late.

4. (Optional) Click on the element for more details to extend it Click Details view.

For more ways to test your work status and monitor your work, go to see for a class at your work.

5.3 Connecting with Your Classmates

- **Post to the class stream**

If your teacher allows, you can use postings, comments, and replies to communicate with your class on the Stream page.

1. A post is a piece of knowledge or query that you add to a stream of the class. (For example: When are we going to visit the Museum?)

2. A comment is a response to a message or a comment. (For instance: We're going next Friday)

3. An answer is an answer to a statement by someone who discusses them. (For example, Thanks to the name + commenter!)

Not all teachers on the Stream page allow for updates and comments.

Note: You can submit a private message to your teacher about an assignment or question if you don't want to add to the Stream list.

Create a post:

To ask a question or exchange details with your teacher and classmates, build a message.

1. Go to the classroom.google.com.

2. Click on the link.

3. Click on the Share something with your class on the Stream tab.

Note: If you can't see Share anything with your class, your instructor has shut off posting permissions.

4. Enter what you want to say, and then press Mail.

- **Use +mention to share messages**

If, when you submit a post in the Classroom, you want to capture somebody's attention, use '+' or '@' with the person's email to mention them. You may include '+' or '@' classmates or your instructor, or both, in-class stream comments or answers to invite them to enter a discussion or show your post.

For example, you can send your answer when your teacher posts a question, and also + mention a classmate to enter your discussion with your teacher.

When you use the '+' or '@' sign to name someone in your comment or reply, the person you listed will receive an email if they have alerts set up in their account settings.

Note mentions '+' or '@' only function in the class line.

+ To address someone

1. Go to the classroom.google.com.

2. Click on the link.

3. Write a message in the comment box Add class or, if you are making a new post, in the class box Post.

4. Enter + or @ and an autocomplete list of classmates appears when you type the person's name.

5. Press Enter to pick the first name and add the email address to the sector.

Scroll down the list to pick a name, and press Enter to pick a specific name.

6. Click the Mail icon.

Note: If the name you want is not shown in the Auto-Complete list form in the full email address

- **Send an email**

In the Classroom, you could contact your teachers and classmates.

> 1. Use your school account to give us an email. This account is also known as a Training account for the G Suite. See about Classroom user accounts to learn about your account form.
>
> 2. The school admin will turn on the email. In the Classroom, on the People page, the admin has turned off an email if you don't see Email next to a name.

- **Share to Classroom from a mobile device**

You can attach webpages from your mobile device to new tasks, questions, or updates in a class, without having to leave the page that you share. You can build a new assignment without going to the Classroom first if you see the Share to Classroom on a web page. Like the other social media icons on the website, you can consider Link to Classroom.

On your computer, you can share links, photos, pictures, and items from Google Drive into the Classroom.

1. Tap More Share Classroom on the website, connect, photo, or picture.

2. The latter active class is selected by default. Tap Next to pick another class to modify the class.

3. Tap which sort of post you would like to use.

5. Tap Post. Complete the task, issue, or announcement.

Chapter 6: Additional Tips for Using Google Classroom

Google Classroom streamlines student-work management announcements, assignment, selection, marking, reviews, and return. It has saved work hours for many teachers.

Digital work grading can be tedious without a robust workflow and a certain strategy. Google Classroom makes it more effective to work with students if you understand how Classroom works and how to use it to get the benefit. A few fast tips can often make all the difference.

- **Use move to top to bring relevant older material back to students' attention**

This simple act bumps the top of the class stream with an assignment, announcement, or request. You are using this if students have not turned up an assignment in OR if you want to remind them of a deadline to come.

- **Use the right kind of comment**

There are different kinds of comments you can leave in the Classroom for students. Knowing how each one works will increase productivity and effectiveness.

- **Adding user comments:**

Do so by adding a comment on the "outside" of an assignment or notification in your user stream. This will make the statement available to the entire class (vital if it's an answer to a problem that everybody may have).

- **Adding private comments:**

This is achieved by showing student results and clicking on the document. The comment bar at the bottom on the right, where you can see student submissions, adds a message that only the student can see (vital if it has sensitive grade information or feedback).

- **Add notes in the doc / slide / sheet / drawing:**

Do so by clicking on the file that the student sent to you. After highlighting something you wish to comment on, press the black speech bubble button. This provides a very pointed statement on specific things in student work (important for feedback to be very exact).

- **Use announcements to share "right now" links**

Advertisements place content in the classroom stream without the need for students to hand in an assignment. Using them to provide vital connections, docs/files, and videos for students that they will need right now. (If this is a resource that they will often need, add that resource to the "About" tab instead.)

- **Reuse posts**

In the classroom stream, advertisers put material without the students having to hand in an assignment. Using them to provide the students with critical links, docs/files, and videos they'll need right now. (If this is a tool they also use, add the device instead of to the 'About' tab.)

- **Grade everything in one place**

In the top left of the Classroom, press the three lines button, and pick "Work" at the right. Here you can find all the assignments in one place for all of your classes. Work your way according to the list and get at one spot on top of everything.

- **Email all students in the "Students" tab**

Once you click on the "Students" category, select the checkbox above everything to highlight everything students. Click "Actions" and "Email." This is nice to call special attention to what you want to communicate to students OR to communicate in a longer form.

- **Using the keyboard instead of the mouse.**

Beat moving keyboard commands and press the cursor through time. Google Classroom's best one: When entering classes, type the grade for the assignment of a specific student, then press the down key to hit the next student. Loop with keystrokes instead of mouse clicks by students to save lots of time.

- **Get Classroom emails the way you want.**

Do you spend too much time deleting Classroom email alerts and wish you could switch them off? At the top left of the Classroom, press the three lines button, and select "Settings" at the bottom. There is a checkbox that permits you to turn off email notifications. (Or if you shut it off and wish you could get texts, that's where you shut it on!)

- **Get the features you like in the Classroom.**

Have you any ideas for a new function in Google Classroom? You can do it but wish you could do it more relaxed? That type of feedback is what teachers want from the Google Classroom team. Tap on the? "Click at the end of the bottom left of the screen and pick 'Send Feedback.' According to a member of the Google Classroom team who spoke to my Google Teacher Academy community in December 2014, somebody in their team reads every single feedback item sent that way. It's how they have made all of the big improvements to Google Classroom apps. And the more common a request for a feature, the more likely it will be put into effect. So give reviews, and always give it!

- **Create a Class and Add Students**

You may display all the students in your class in the Students section. You can manually connect students to your class, or you can use your own Google account to enter your class by yourself. Google Classroom gives you a class code located on the left side of the screen when developing a class. Share the class code with the students that you'd like to enter. Students sign into their Google Accounts from their phones, tablets, or Chrome books and use the class code to enter.

You will also decide within the Student section whether your students can comment on the comments, announcements, and assignments you are making or whether they can only share. When you wish, you can also opt to be the only one in your class who can post and blog.

You'll find the tasks, updates, and questions you make in the Stream section. It is the area you'll be spending much of your time after setting up your classes. Read below for information on Google Classroom assignments, questions, and announcements.

- **Using Google Classroom Assignments:**

Assignments are a perfect way to collect student work and get reviews and grades from the students. When you make an assignment, you should include detailed instructions, due dates, and a subject for that assignment. If you have a due date for the assignment, the students will have to apply their work for that assignment before 11:59 PM on the day. Unless they send the job late, the task is still approved by Google Classroom, but it means that it was turned in late.

Google Classroom Assignments, one of the best features, is that you can add files to the assignments you make. You can add a new file from your computer, a Google Drive file, a video from YouTube, or a link to a Website. One concept is that a teacher in business education may give a written prompt to a particular person in the news and add a link to that individual's YouTube video delivering a speech.

Students can upload files of any kind to your Classroom, not just to Google Docs. Not only can students apply for their completed work as files, but you can open and grade them directly from the Classroom right there. You can access files sent to your Classroom as long as your machine has an Internet connection and the program required to open the file. You don't even need to be on your machine from school!

For instance, you can assign an essay, and your students can submit their completed essays from a computer that has a good Internet connection to an assignment you created in your Google Classroom. You can then open the file at school or home, and store it on your computer. Google Classroom for assignments functions like a "Dropbox." Students don't have to print their work anymore and hand it directly to you. This gives you more time to concentrate on going forward during training, as opposed to spending time gathering work.

- **Spark Discussions with the Feature:**

Google Classroom Questions enable you to ask a question in a particular class. As with assignments, you can add new files to the questions you submit, and if you wish, you can attach a due date. In the Classroom, you can post short response questions or multiple-choice questions for your students to the response.

As students answer a question of multiple-choice, Google Classroom tabulates the results for that question and shows you the breakdown in real-time of the answers from the students. When you click on one of the answers to multiple choices, the Classroom will indicate which students have chosen that option.

When students answer a short answer question, the results cannot be tabulated by Google Classroom, so it simply displays answers from the students. You may comment or respond to each student at that level, and give them a grade as you see fit.

- **Advertisements to Your Students:**

In addition to creating new assignments and questions, Google Classroom helps you to create advertisements. Students can respond to your announcements and, by creating a line, you can answer back. The whole class can have one announcement-based conversation. Again you have the option to add an announcement file, a YouTube video, or a connection.

Advertisements are a perfect way to post updates to the students about assignment due dates. You can also plan to post updates at a later date, which will help you and your students remain coordinated.

- **Why will Google Classroom be used in Middle School Elective Courses?**

What we find most convincing regarding Google Classroom is that it enables you to interact more beyond the classroom with your students. Before students at Google Classroom had to be in the classroom physically for you to ask them a question. You can do it any time now. Students can likewise send work from anywhere they have access to the Internet. That saves a lot of time for those of us who teach middle school elective courses when you think of how many students, we may have during the school year!

Google Classroom saves time and paper, and allows you to create lessons easily, post assignments, and interact with students. It also allows you to check which students have completed their assignments, so you can provide direct input so grades in real-time. Essentially, Google Classroom positions all of the assignments, announcements, and student research in one place.

Whatever subject you're teaching, Google Classroom is a fantastic way to exchange knowledge with your students, collect their work, and provide input. If you have a Google Account with your school, the Classroom will just sit there waiting to help you educate your students and engage them.

Are you ready to teach your google students?

- **Google Classroom supports sequenced learning for anyone:**

Particularly during remote-only work, Google Classroom and G Suite applications may support learning needs for all kinds of organizations. Google Classroom may be used by any company that uses G Suite: it is not restricted to schools. The classroom allows a viable choice to help a teacher lead any group of individuals through a set of organized topics and tasks. Although an instructor with a collection of students will always use the Classroom, the same method can also be used for professional development efforts.

- **Understand context**

Trying to understand the meaning of the student before attempting to express material. Students may face difficulties not usually present in a school classroom, including in-household children of certain ages, adults who may also be home, and a physical setting not generally structured to facilitate learning. In the degree practicable, take the time to make sure every one of the students understands the meaning and circumstances.

- **Enable offline work:**

Change assignments to allow students to work offline, as not every student will have access to a home internet connection. Recent reports indicate that "15 percent of U.S. households with school-age children do not have high-speed internet service at home." Provide access to downloaded content rather than streaming them. You can, for example, record a video (e.g., with Hangouts Meet) then upload it to Google Classroom instead of connecting it to a YouTube video. You could also have an article that you would like students to read as a PDF or Google Doc, rather than a web link.

Try an EPUB edition if you intend to teach with a very long text, which allows the reader greater control over fonts, font size, and line spacing. A student can download and store items to Google Drive for offline access, including a video file, a PDF, or Google Docs, Sheets, or Slides.

- **Verify whether an assignment can be rendered on a mobile device:**

Preferably, you can also test to make sure whether-assignment can be done on an Android phone, iPhone, or on a laptop in Chrome. For instance, most assignments involving the use of Google Docs, Papers, or Slides will work well, as those apps not only work well in a browser but can also be installed on Android and iOS devices.

The Docs, Boards, and Slides apps currently differ slightly by the platform. Support for add-ons (in Docs, Sheets, and Slides), drop-down lists (in Google Sheets), and audio or video files inserted (in Google Slides), for example, vary. In every G Suite app on Android, iOS, or Chrome on the web, not every feature function the same way, so it helps check new assignments and tasks.

If you don't have access to the three platforms checking your assignment (i.e., Android, iOS, Chrome), contact the tech support team at your school. A well-run IT support department is likely to be able to arrange a time to help you check that any device can complete an assignment.

Also, if your company provides students with a computer, I urge you to create platform-neutral assignments to optimize the students' ability to achieve a mission, regardless of the system. Recall always testing assignments for any third-party applications that you are using.

- **Join the discussion Twitter:**

Thousands of teachers who care about online communication and sharing tools on Twitter every day. Google invites people to use the hashtag # teach from home, but there are also a lot of excellent tools.

- **Include learning goals in each listed activity or assignment**

This is not so much a comforting case, as it is a fantastic pedagogy. It will always send you back to the unit plan or the regular curricular, keeping you grounded. And reminding students what the purpose of increasing learning activity is will always be present.

"Why are we doing this?".

- **Get a fast sense of the progress of your students.**

You often post your self-assessments in Google Classroom, particularly in Math Units. They are an easy but effective way for me to gather data on the learning and success of my students, which will guide my next steps.

You get those results by posting a multiple-choice question right in the Classroom. Click on any button, and you'll see which students selected the skill level.

- **Share Homeroom Classrooms with all specialist teachers**

Encourage your language teachers, art teachers, and band teachers to drop announcements and resources into their classrooms. Yeah, your band instructor will have their own Google Classroom system for your students in the homeroom. Even if they don't, a better option is getting access to your Classroom.

- **Post to several Classrooms once**

If you're a specialist teacher, use this tool. You don't have to post different assignments in each Classroom. All related Classrooms are updated at once.

- **Change Google Classroom notifications to mute Classroom emails and alerts that do not belong to you**

After sharing the two previous strategies on sharing Google Classrooms, this technique is essential. Switch off Classroom Updates you don't teach.

When you do not take this measure, you will receive email updates from each resubmission of assignments or any private comment made by each student in each Classroom. Some teachers have access to up to 10 or even more Classrooms at my school. Which makes for a large number of notifications!

By restricting updates to only the classes you teach, you will combat this. With that said, where possible, respond to private comments. Some very good communication for some students might happen there.

- **Structure weekly times to check email inboxes for the homeroom students and arrange classroom assignments**

For most middle and high school students, email is dull. Yet Classroom encourages useful e-mail dialog between teacher and student. In the Classroom, you can post reviews in private comments showing up in the form of an email to students. You may email selected students to remind them to send an assignment, post updates about upcoming events, or post-self-assessment check-ins to track learning. Most of all of those interactions run on email so that students can check their inbox once a week.

We are not going to do it on their own, and we can't ask them to. Each week we have to set aside 15 minutes or more to ensure this life ability is happening.

Some would say email is not going to be around forever, and maybe they are right. But for the last 25 years, it has been operating well, so it will not be going anywhere anytime soon. Make sure the students are learning how to maximize the inbox.

- **Build a school-wide Google Classroom**

This allows for school-wide polls, debates, hot lunch order form submissions, student photo submissions for the yearbook, delivery of announcements, etc. Full disclosure: I'm not utilizing this — partially to slow down the influx of ideas, I'm imposing on colleagues in a new teaching group. But at a corresponding school, I set this up, and it works wonderfully.

- **For managers: build a Google Classroom for staff members, with managers becoming members and teachers becoming students**

It is a perfect way to reduce email traffic. Conduct fast and effective surveys of workers. Post "assignments" such as plans for professional development, and require "students" (teachers) to apply when completed. Or post reporting tools and open commentaries so that teachers can view posts as boards of discussion.

Classroom on Google. It's not a tremendous mind-blowing, but it works. To get the most out of Google Classroom, optimize your time and resources, and better serve your learners, adopt these techniques.

Conclusion

Google Classroom is Google's online learning platform enabling teachers and students to do their daily lessons remotely in the classroom. Teachers can now monitor classes, build tasks, organize lesson notes and lesson plans with Google Classroom, and even score each student on-line.

You will find a full guide inside this book, which will teach you how to use Google Classroom effectively. This guide aims to explore and show you how to optimize all the functionality of this google service.

If we could give something to teachers that would save them time, save the money from teaching, interact more with students and parents, support struggling with learners, and improve students' learning environment, will they consider using it? We hope they will.

If you've been using Google Classroom for the last couple of years, you're probably already "sold" on why it's nice to use it. But if it's new to you, you're possibly curious to learn why this move is beneficial for students.

Google Classroom is a free, integrated learning platform offering both students and teachers a range of benefits. If you're a 1:1 class or just rock the machine carts from time to time, Google Classroom will boost efficiency in your classroom and take control of your workflow to the next level.

Google is at the cutting-edge of digital technologies, and what online services people want. An online classroom program gives schools and individuals who just want to send others knowledge a place to do so without investing a lot of money. The free productivity tools also give you a space for organizing classes and storing documents.

Google Classroom streamlines the entire education cycle by removing the need for papers to be scanned and copied and entering grades manually into a grade book. Instead, it all happens online, saving time and energy. Teachers often save time and may focus on individual learning.

You can connect webpages from your mobile device to new tasks, questions, or updates in a class, without having to leave the page that you share. You can build a new assignment without going to the Classroom first if you see the Share to Classroom on a web page. Like the other social media icons on the website, you can consider Link to Classroom.

Many elective middle school teachers are looking for resources and tools to save time and make their lives easier. Often the process of organizing student work takes up a significant portion of your class time and ensuring that your students are aware of upcoming assignments. A lot of teachers have begun using Google Classroom as a way to organize classrooms better.

If you have a G Suite Education (previously Google Apps for Education) account in your district, you may want to look at setting up and maintaining Google Classrooms for all of your students.

Teachers have been switching online classes because of the coronavirus pandemic as schools, colleges, and universities closed campuses. This transition tested the willingness of many teachers to adapt content and practices during the pandemic while at home-often with other family members. Luckily, schools using G Suite have access to Google Classroom, a cloud-based program that lets teachers build and manage classes, classwork, grades, and student communication.

Google has created a new website, Teach from Home, in response to the COVID-19 crisis explicitly designed to help teachers adapt to online courses. The website offers links to tutorials to help teachers develop experience with different G Suite teaching resources.

If you're a teacher, a student, or even a relative, maybe you've heard of that. Google Classroom is a step in the good direction for classroom technology, and there's a reason so many students and teachers use it. If you've been wondering how, or even just what, to use Google Classroom, you're in luck.

And a whole lot more. You will be shocked by how this benefits students, even while there are teachers who usually aren't going to want to use it right away because it's a new piece of technology. It's superbly helpful for students and teachers. It's the ideal tool to use if you're trying to create an engaging and very positive learning atmosphere because, in turn, you're going to be able to interact more with students, let them know about announcements because improvements, and create the best classroom environment for yourself and other students.

Technology has come a long way; Google Classroom allows you to use this to create a better learning experience for yourself, and others as well, so that progress can be created.

Reference

Common Sense Education. n.d. *Teachers' Essential Guide To Google Classroom | Common Sense Education*. [online] Available at: <https://www.commonsense.org/education/articles/teachers-essential-guide-to-google-classroom>.

Educational Technology and Mobile Learning. n.d. *Google Classroom: The Basics For Teachers And Students*. [online] Available at: <https://www.educatorstechnology.com/2019/02/google-classroom-basics-for-teachers.html>.

Learning, T., YouTube, A., Market, H., Companies, 1., Vetting, A., Skills, I., As Schools Unveil New Tech Initiatives, K., Campus, W., Research, P. and Program, U., n.d. *10 Benefits Of Google Classroom Integration - The Tech Edvocate*. [online] The Tech Edvocate. Available at: <https://www.thetechedvocate.org/10-benefits-of-google-classroom-integration/>.

Ditch That Textbook. n.d. *10 Tips To Use Google Classroom Effectively And Efficiently - Ditch That Textbook*. [online] Available at: <https://ditchthattextbook.com/10-tips-to-use-google-classroom-effectively-and-efficiently/>.

Getting Smart. n.d. *6 Reasons Why Google Classroom Is A Great Tool For Teachers*. [online] Available at: <https://www.gettingsmart.com/2016/11/6-reasons-google-classroom-great-tool/>.

Reviews.financesonline.com. n.d. *Google Classroom Reviews: Pricing & Software Features 2020 - Financesonline.Com*. [online] Available at: <https://reviews.financesonline.com/p/google-classroom/>.

Teachthought.com. n.d. [online] Available at: <https://www.teachthought.com/current-events/changes-new-features-in-google-classroom/>.

November, n.d. *7 Hurdles To Overcome To Get The Most Out Of Technology*. [online] Technology Solutions That Drive Education. Available at: <https://edtechmagazine.com/k12/article/2006/10/7-hurdles-overcome-get-most-out-technology>.

GoGuardian Help Center. n.d. *Add Students To A Classroom*. [online] Available at: <https://help.goguardian.com/hc/en-us/articles/115004032403-Add-Students-to-a-Classroom>.

EdTechTeam. n.d. *How To Create Your First Google Classroom - Edtechteam*. [online] Available at: <https://www.edtechteam.com/blog/2019/11/how-to-create-your-first-google-classroom/>.

Google Classroom 2020

An Easy Guide on How to Teach Digitally in 2020 and To Manage Your Google Classroom Effectively

Introduction

Education is essential for making one's life easier. It is undoubtedly the primary tool for improving one's life. A child's education starts at home. It is a lifelong cycle that does not end until one's death. Education undoubtedly defines the quality of a person's life. It strengthens one's awareness, abilities, and improves attitude and personality. Perhaps remarkable of all, education impacts people's chances of work. A highly educated person is likely to get a good job, as well. The drive for universal literacy is a phenomenon of the last 150–200 years. Traditionally, schools for young people have been accompanied by specialized training for priests, administrators, and experts. Monasteries associated with the Roman Catholic Church were the centers of education and literacy throughout the Early Middle Ages, preserving the selection of the church from Latin learning and retaining the art of writing. Until their formal establishment, many medieval universities were run for hundreds of years as Christian monastic schools, where monks taught classes, and later as cathedral schools, evidence of those later university's immediate precursors in many places dates back to the early 6th century. In the 6th and 7th centuries, the Gundishapur Academy, initially the Sassanid empire's intellectual hub and subsequently a Muslim learning center, offered medicine, philosophy, theology, and science training. The staff was not only versed in Zoroastrian and Persian cultures but also Greek and Indian studies. The education that we acquire today is certainly different from that of our primitive ancestors. The teaching methodologies, the concepts, and the means of providing education have evolved through time. The entire paradigm has shifted.

Initially, education passed down from the forefathers to their children-particularly the sons, so that they could carry forward the rituals and assist in their work. Their mode of learning was probably harsher, where they had to walk so many miles to get to their places of learning. Nevertheless, they had no option. Until today, physical classes have been prevalent. In this form of education, one has to leave their house and get to the educational institute to be taught. Although this form of learning could never go out of trend, because of some of its prominent benefits, it still is being replaced, to a large extent, by the online classroom learning. In online classes, one gets to learn at the comfort of their home. It is mainly due to the factors such as time and cost of traveling to faraway areas for learning, that the online classes have been introduced. Lack of attention in physical classes, potential bullying in schools and colleges, geographical immobility followed by a desire to learn various cultures being in a single place could be some other reasons. Live online lessons are similar in some respects to conventional face-to-face classes — an instructor can deliver information and communicate with a group of people in real-time — in other respects, some significant differences do exist. The first notable difference is the management of classrooms. The teacher is free to push the learners around in a physical environment, grouping them in various ways and setting out the class in a way that will ensure that the lessons run smoothly. Most online courses use conferencing software that allows for breakout groups and various learner configurations in the classroom.

Another distinction is the use of back channels. In educational contexts, such as seminars, back channels are especially common where the audience is forced to sit and listen for a more extended period. During the past, lecturers frequently banned cell phones from the lecture halls, but today, as a backchannel for the audience, progressive lecturers may also set up a twitter hashtag. Online classrooms usually have a text feature built into them, which the audience may take as a backchannel to ensure that they are engaged. Lack of visual feedback in online classes is a growing problem that teachers face. While talking directly to an audience in the same space, presentations can customize according to the audience's visual input. A room full of uninterested faces is a sure sign to a presenter or teacher that a more engaging activity needs to be added or their presentation- modified to engage the audience more. A cleverer presenter in the online classroom will make good use of the available resources to get similar feedback. Daily questions to the audience that they can answer using voting tools are a valuable way of ensuring whether the participants are participating in a live online session.

To sum up, although there are variations between physical and online learning, both delivery methods can be utilized in the hands of a well-trained instructor to accomplish the same goals. The chosen mode of teaching depends as much on the logistics of providing your training as on the subject being taught. However, live online lessons are becoming an increasingly apparent option for any professional development program in an increasingly globalized world. E-learning platforms have become even more crucial in the year 2020 when the world as a whole is stuck in the middle of a global pandemic, i.e., coronavirus, and people cannot leave their houses due to the lockdown situation. Under such circumstances, applications such as Google classrooms come to the rescue!

Chapter 1: Introduction to Online Classrooms

Online education is exhibiting an upward trend, specifically in the current year 2020. A recent study showed that 46 percent of new graduates take online credit as part of their degree, as more people shift to hybrid courses that combine distance learning with conventional classroom approaches than ever before. Most students are drawn to online learning versatility and combine their studies with work or personal commitments. Among some, a less costly alternative to conventional campus-based courses is distance learning. A three-year undergraduate degree will cost up to $50,000, while postgraduate courses can bring back around $5,000 for a student. And although online learning courses prices differ very significantly, comparable degrees cost around 50 percent less.

Many experts say the future of education is in online learning. If technology becomes more prevalent, more and more students can gain exposure to the kind of information that can significantly boost their job opportunities and maybe even enhance the planet. Online learning will allow students in developing countries to study topics such as coding, computer programming, and engineering and thus drive innovation around the globe.

Providing online courses and blended learning for many universities can play a crucial role in their long-term survival. Most students are covered by high tuition fees associated with full-time, campus-based classes.

Studying full-time challenges other essential responsibilities for others, such as a current career or raising a young family. After that, universities offering online learning services allow more students to enroll in their schools, including those residing in regional areas or, in some cases, in a different country. Any large organization must keep up with market demand, and rising technology and universities are no exception. Online learning, in other words, is not only here to stay; it is going to become an essential part of the future.

Besides, the online teaching approaches are already being introduced into the classroom by schools and higher education institutions, including innovations of the next decade, such as augmented reality, AI, and virtual reality. More than six million students have already had their VR-based classes, which involves virtual field trips to famous historical sites such as the Roman Coliseum, according to a tech-based study.

Meanwhile, companies around the world are developing with Google, a range of VR products that will allow virtual experiments to be performed by science students. One project involves a VR game in which a forensic science student will be able to examine and analyze the evidence they find in a virtual crime scene.

These innovations inevitably lead to wilder forms of speculation, but the emphasis on convergence rather than total replacement is essential to note in schools and big tech.

In other words, teachers in real life will always play a critical role in educating the next generation of students. They are essential.

Traditional classroom-based methods of teaching will still have a room, but even these are being combined with online learning.

And though predicting in which directions technology will take us in is almost impossible, online learning is expected to become a big part of educational institutions all over the world.

This approach is even more worthwhile in the current year when a coronavirus badly takes the world. Learning has been affected adversely, all around the world. About 185 countries have shut down their schools and universities, according to UNESCO. Education for hundreds of millions of children and young people has been affected. Education providers are trying to take up the task of teaching at a distance. Parents are working out their position, and teachers are doing their best in an ambivalent way.

Approximately 5.4 million South Korean primary, middle and high school students begin a single academic year in 2020 by distance learning, as the country aims to counter the COVID-19 pandemic.

One major problem is that certain places, colleges, and students are not equipped with the resources required to take part in these classes. Up to 85,000, students need devices such as tablets or laptops to take online courses, according to the Korean Ministry of Education. According to their ministry of education, it will purchase in excess, thus investing around 1.5 billion South Koreans won ($1.2 million) to upgrade some rural schools' wireless internet networks. The truth is that this is the moment of fame of online learning!

1.1 What is Online Learning?

Online learning is an education taking place over the Internet. In other words, it's sometimes referred to as "e-learning." Online learning, however, is only one form of "distance learning" - the paragliding term for any learning that takes place over a distance and not in a typical classroom.

Online education or distance learning is education for those students who may not always be physically present in a school.

Traditionally, this usually included correspondence courses in which the student connected to the classroom by e-mail. Today, it is about online education. A distance learning program can either be ultimately distance learning, or a mixture of remote learning and conventional classroom instruction (called hybrid or blended). Massive open online courses (MOOCs), providing large-scale interactive participation and free access via the World Wide Web or other network technologies, are new modes of education in distance learning.

In a typical classroom, you also learn through listening, reading, writing, and doing other things that your teacher has designed. Online courses are different in the sense that the professor or other students are not in the same place. You'll probably never meet in person with your teacher or fellow students.

Students "attend" class in online courses by accessing the class web pages. According to the class schedule, they complete their assignments. Students use e-mail and online discussion boards to connect with the professor and their classmates. With busy schedules, this class structure is extremely versatile. Students will frequently log in to the course at any time of day (or evening). Being successful requires programming skills and determination. Students need typing skills and must be able to write to understand.

Difference between online and Distance Learning

Although all of these teaching approaches include the use of a computer or other gadgets by the students, there are some variations between them, i.e., online learning, as well as distance learning, need similar online learning resources, but the similarity ends there.

Generally, there are three main differences between online and Distance Learning:

- Location
- Interaction
- Intention

Location Differences

The primary distinction between online learning and distance learning is the location. Online learning or e-learning allows students to be with the teacher in the classroom while working through their interactive digital lessons and tests. However, students work remotely at home while the teacher assigns the assignments and digitally checks in while they use distance learning.

Interaction variations

Due to location variations, the relationship between teachers and their students often varies. Online learning can require daily in-person contact between teachers and students. This is because online learning, along with other teaching techniques, is used as a blended learning technique. Distance learning, however, involves no contact between teachers and students in-person. Nonetheless, you'll probably rely on digital communication channels such as messaging apps, video calls, discussion boards, and the Learning Management System (LMS) for your school.

Differences in Intention

The intent of the teaching technique is the final difference between online and distance learning. Online learning is intended to be used in conjunction with several other diverse methods of teaching in-person.

It's a supplementary way to change things up in your classroom and provide your students with a range of learning experiences. Distance learning is a technique for providing instructions solely electronically, not as a difference in the teaching style.

Each has a role in education at the end of day-online learning or distance learning. Depending on the needs of teachers and students, one will be better than the other. Online Learning works best for teachers in middle and high schools who want to provide their students with new forms of learning. Usually, distance learning fits better for older students who have constant exposure to technology at home and who work independently on their own.

1.2 History of Online Education

In 1728, one of the earliest attempts for remote learning was made public. It was in the Boston Gazette for "Caleb Philipps, Instructor of the New Method of Short Hand," pursuing students who wished to learn by weekly mailed lessons. In the 1840s, Sir Isaac Pitman offered the first distance education course in the modern sense, offering a method of shorthand through mailing texts transcribed into shorthand on postcards and collecting transcriptions from his students in exchange for rectification. The aspect of student feedback was a key advancement in Pitman's system. This scheme was made possible by the implementation of standardized postal rates throughout England in 1840.

This early beginning proved extremely popular, and the Phonographic Correspondence Society was established three years later to develop these courses more formally. The Society cleared the way for the later establishment of Sir Isaac Pitman Colleges around the country.

The Society to Promote Studies at Home, established in 1873, was the first correspondence school in the United States. Established in 1894, Wolsey Hall, Oxford was the first distance learning college in the UK.

Correspondence courses from universities

The University of London became the first institution to offer distance learning degrees, finding its External Program in 1858. The backdrop to this move was that the college (later known as University College London) was non-denominational, and there was an uproar against the "godless" university in light of the strong theological rivalries at the time. The question soon came down to which institutions had degree-granting powers and which ones did not. The adjusting solution that emerged in 1836 was that the sole authority to administer the exams leading to degrees should be granted to a new officially recognized agency called the "University of London." It would serve as an examination body for the University of London colleges, originally including King's College London and University College London, while granting degrees to the students for the University of London. With the State granting examination powers to a separate body, the groundwork was laid for the formation of a system within the new university that would conduct both exams and grant qualifications to students enrolled in some other institution or those following up self-study.

It was referred to by Charles Dickens as "People's University" because it offered access to higher education for students from less privileged backgrounds.

The External System was chartered by Queen Victoria in 1858, enabling the University of London to be the first one to offer remote learning degrees to students. Established in 1888 to train immigrant coal miners to become state mine inspectors or foremen, it enrolled 2,500 new students in 1894 and enrolled 72,000 new students in 1895. In 1906 gross registrations reached 900,000. The rise was due to the use of 1200 aggressive in-person sales clerks, sending out full textbooks instead of single lessons.

In the 19th century, education became a high priority, as American high schools and colleges greatly grew. Night schools were opened for people who were older or too busy with family obligations, such as the YMCA school in Boston, which became North-eastern University. Private correspondence schools outside the major cities provided a versatile, narrowly oriented solution. Large companies systematized their training programs for new workers. The Business Schools National Association grew from 37 in 1913, to 146 in 1920. In the early 1880s, private schools were opened across the country that provided advanced technical training to all those who studied, not just one company's employees.

Beginning in Milwaukee in 1907, public schools started to offer free training programs. In 1920, about one-third of the American population lived in towns of 100,000 or more; communication methods needed to be introduced to meet the remainder.

Australia was particularly involved with its large distances; in 1911, the University of Queensland established its Department of Correspondence Studies.

The University of South Africa, located in South Africa, previously an examination and testing body, began to teach distance education in 1946. The first meeting of the International Conference on Correspondence Education was held in 1938. The objective was to provide an individualized education for students at low cost, using a pedagogy of measuring, tracking, classification, and differentiation. Since then, the organization has been called the International Council for Open and Distance Education (ICDE) with headquarters in Oslo, Norway.

Open Universities

The United Kingdom Open University was created based on Michael Young's dream, by the then Labour Government headed by Prime Minister Harold Wilson. Planning started in 1965 under the Minister of State for Education, Jennie Lee, who set up an Open University (OU) model to expand access to the highest levels of higher education scholarship. A planning committee was set up, headed by Sir Peter Venables, consisting of university vice-chancellors, educationalists, and television broadcasters. Then, the British Broadcasting Corporation (BBC) Assistant Director of Engineering, James Redmond, had earned much of his training at night school. His inborn vigor for the project did much to solve the technological challenges of using television to transmit teaching programs. As well as research in other fields, it had been at the forefront of developing new technologies to enhance the distance learning service. In January 1969, Walter Perry was appointed first vice-chancellor of the OU, with Anastasios Christodoulou as its founding secretary.

The appointment of the Conservative government under Edward Heath's leadership in 1970 led to budget cuts under Chancellor Iain Macleod of the Exchequer (who had earlier called the concept of an open university a "blithering nonsense"). However, in 1971, the OU admitted the first 25,000 students, embracing a progressive free admission policy. Then, the total student population of traditional universities in the United Kingdom was around 130,000. Athabasca University, Canada's Open University, was found in 1970 and followed a similar trend, albeit independently developed. The Open University inspired the development of

Spain's National University of Distance Education (1972) and Fern University, Germany. Some open universities have evolved into mega-universities, a word that denotes the institutions with more than 100,000 students.

1.3 Different Types of Online Classrooms

Training online comes in several ways. Modern classrooms are available and offer online activities. There are classrooms outside the school building, which are entirely online. And there are options for mixed classrooms which fall in between somewhere.

Internet technology has made many ways of distance learning possible through open educational tools and services, such as e-learning and MOOCs. Although Internet expansion blurs the borders, distance education technologies are divided into two delivery modes: synchronous Learning and asynchronous Learning.

All participants in synchronous learning are "there" at the same time. In this way, it parallels conventional teaching approaches in the classroom, given the remote position of the participants.

This needs setting a timetable. Web conferences, videoconferencing, educational television, instructional television are examples of synchronous technology such as direct-to-broadcast satellite (DBS), internet radio, live streaming, telephone, and online-based VoIP.

Web conferencing software helps promote meetings in distance learning courses and typically provides additional networking resources such as text chat, polling, hand radio. Such tools also facilitate asynchronous engagement by enabling students to listen to synchronous session recordings.

Immersive worlds were often used to improve the participation of the participants in distance education courses.

Another type of synchronous learning that has entered the classroom over the past few years is the use of robot proxies, including those which enable sick students to attend classes. Some universities have started using robot proxies to create more engaging synchronous hybrid classes where students, both remote and in-person, can be present and interact using telerobotics. Remote students sit in front of a table or desk. They use telepresence robots instead of using a computer on the wall.

In asynchronous learning, learners view course materials flexibly according to their schedules. Students don't need to be together concurrently. Mail communication, which is the oldest method of distance education, is an asynchronous delivery system, and so are message board forums, e-mail, video and audio recordings, print materials, voicemail, and fax.

Many courses provided by both open universities and a growing number of campus-based institutions use periodic residential or day teaching sessions to complement distance-based sessions.

Recently, this form of mixed distance and campus-based education has been called "mixed learning" or less frequently "hybrid learning." Most open universities use a blend of technology and a variety of learning modalities (face-to-face, distance, and hybrid) all under the "distance learning" rubric.

Interactive radio and audio instruction (IRI) and (IAI), electronic virtual environments, video sports, webinars, and webcasts are often referred to as e-learning.

As for the forms of online courses, you can hear several different terms. Below are various concepts that may help standardize what is being referred to when looking at the many different online course choices.

Flipped course: Here, instructors record their lectures or use open-source tools to deliver content for the lecture. Students will be able to view the videos and complete a brief assessment of their comprehension of the material before attending class. A prominent benefit of this strategy is that at a time that works best for them, students complete the requisite training at their own pace and, the instructor acts as a facilitator during class, coaching, advising, answering questions, and dealing with misconceptions in real-time. The class will begin with a series of mini-lectures, further explaining material considered difficult or confusing by the students. The rest of the class is focused on active learning, and students and teachers connect. Many "flipped teachers" assume the most significant feature of the flipped paradigm is this. This classroom model is also referred to as an "inverted course."

Hybrid course: A large portion of the course learning process was transferred online in "hybrid" classes, allowing the amount of time spent in the classroom to be cut down. Standard face-to-face training is reduced but not eliminated. It is also called a "blended course."

Face-to-face: A traditional classroom setting where the students and the teacher meet synchronously in the same room; often referred to as "on-ground" or "on-campus" teaching.

Web-based: These classes are most often referred to as online classes, and the term "web-based" is more often used when referencing online classes. Online/Web-based classes typically use an LMS (Canvas, Blackboard, Moodle, etc.) to post instructors' syllabuses, materials, assignments, and communication. Most online courses are self-paced, and others have a unique test and task deadlines.

Web-Enhanced: In this specific course, there is a meeting in the classroom, which is much like a conventional class. There is a teacher at the usual every day, time, and place. Seat time is not replaced, so you will be able to navigate components of your course anytime using a Learning Management System (LMS) like Canvas. Online activities differ from teacher specifications and course specifications. Ideally, the professor will explain expectations on the first day of class, and students will have the flexibility to use an LMS, just as they do with any other technology.

Peer Instruction: Born in Harvard, Peer Instruction incorporates students during a lecture in their learning, and focuses their attention on the basic concepts. Conceptual questions, called ConcepTests, are interspersed with lectures, designed to highlight common difficulties in understanding the subject. Students are provided with one to two minutes to focus on the question and formulate their responses; they then spend two to three minutes debating their responses in groups of three to four, attempting to find consensus on the correct response. This method encourages students to think about the arguments being formulated and helps them to test their comprehension of the concepts long before they exit the classroom.

MOOC: A MOOC (Massive Open Online Course) is an online course designed for public participation on a wide scale and open enrolment. MOOCs are developed by university instructors and give students who are enrolled at the hosting institution a course credit. MOOCs are usually joint projects of institutions of higher education and consortia, including

Coursera, Udacity, and edX. "Open" students can participate in the course activities and receive content delivered electronically while not receiving credit or direct input from the instructional team. Despite criticism of completion rates, MOOCs are thought to represent a new age of open learning, using network technology to promote interaction between scholar and student groups with no institutional or regional boundaries.

1.4 Various myths about online learning

With the increasing number of online college courses, you may be curious about your choices. Online Learning's simplicity and versatility are appealing, but is that format effective? You don't want the paper that is written on to be worth a degree; you want the skills and credentials that come with a great college program. Your questions can stem from some of the common myths about learning online. If there is some possibility that these misunderstandings are getting in the way of you and your dream future, it is time to bring them to light.

Myth#1 You have to teach yourself everything

Only because you're not physically present in front of your teachers, that doesn't mean they won't be there to provide you with assistance along the way.

Online class teachers have to engage their students and teach them the subject matter, just like in a brick and mortar class. Not attending classes in person can seem like a shortcoming (at first glance). However, professors tend to put extra effort into the instructions for the syllabus, arrangement of units, and assignments so that everything is directed to the maximum level. As in-person courses, when something is not obvious, it is up to the student to ask questions.

Myth#2 There is zero communication with class-fellows

You can utilize technology to speak to a friend face to face around the globe or work with a community of business associates, and you can even use it to communicate with teachers and classmates. Interaction is a fundamental part of most online programs where each student is usually required to post multiple times a week on course forums and occasionally meet with professors once at a time. Some professors and students think the posts at the website are much more interesting than just in-class conversations. Everyone has an opportunity to gather their views in writing and express themselves in their own time and in a more deliberate way than through contact in real-time. You would get a better feeling for who your peers are in a moderated online forum where everyone has to participate than in a lecture hall where only a few students speak up. Online conversations will give people a whole lot more insight. There are rules and etiquette on how to talk, and you'll quickly learn how people feel about a particular topic.

Myth#3 Professors are faceless

Professors often hold office hours in a typical brick-and-mortar university where students can stop by, say hello and

ask questions.

They might also be available after class, or reachable by e-mail, depending on the instructor. Professor does a lot to strengthen the content and help students connect and understand. Professors can link to students via a Facebook program page as well as via their class platforms. The faculty can be very much available. Students could take full advantage of any chance of interacting through social media. You just never know what sorts of friendships both the message boards and social media can create!

Myth #4 You can't build a network

Talking of friendships, the people you meet are one of the undervalued benefits of education—and the connections they can bring into your life. Many people rely on college networks for landing jobs and learning about solid possibilities. That kind of relationship-building could seem hard in an online class at first glance, but the intentionality required in online platforms might make network-building easier. Although that is certainly not true of all online services, diligent counselors and managers (as well as instructors) should have a strong curriculum that can provide job guidance and connections.

Myth #5 Virtual classes are better than on-campus classes

When you are enrolling in an approved program, this is not the case! You may have been a little excited and optimistic reading this misconception that online education will be a better alternative for schooling. According to the professors, students should not only expect online courses to be just as demanding as their counterparts on campus but should also want them to be challenging.

The perceived distance from coursework online makes you feel as though you can put it off. If you're not a self-motivated individual, an online program may be especially challenging. Likewise, compared with conventional classes, online classes are not easier.

Online courses tend to be more challenging and take longer to complete. For student success in an online class, comprehensive reading criteria, and time management are needed for the assignment deadlines. Therefore, never underestimate the time commitment; keep pace and make sure you meet the demands of an online class!

Myth #6 To take online courses, you need to be a tech whiz

You can order a meal from your phone with only a few quick taps on the screen. You post the images and connect on social networks with friends and relatives. Hence, well-built technology doesn't have a learning curve down the steep. And online learning platforms are becoming more complex and equipped for better interactions with the students. Age or technological skill can never be a reason for you not to try learning opportunities online.

Myth #7 Online learning is an all-lecture

Video lectures are a part of many programs, but online learning goes far deeper than that. Online training does require a great deal of practical research. You'll be given tasks in specific online programs that mostly mimic what you're going to do in a real work setting—this offers you the opportunity to apply what you've learned and show your understanding.

Myth #8 Online degrees are not valued by the employers

When online learning was brand new, employers may have been wary—especially in industries where a degree is a non-negotiable qualification, such as education or healthcare. But online learning's popularity has been growing for many years, and what once seemed new is now very common.

The stigma against online degrees is fading as more and more employers, and those with the hiring authority have themselves received degrees online. There are several situations where an employer might also find an online education to be of higher value. Many of the updated technologies used in the offices are replicated in the virtual classes. Communicating and interacting online with colleagues is not unusual, so your online learning experience should prepare you for that interaction as well.

Myth#9 Online classes are all about procrastination

Procrastination does not go well with e-learning. Online class procrastination will cause more problems for the students than usual class procrastination. Students online need to be confident, empowered, and self-starters. Students must be able to set their schedules and observe them. The versatility of an online class needs to be handled by students.

Myth#10 All the work can be crammed into a single login session

Students usually have trouble being successful in a class when they only log in once every week or twice. Some students learn best through studying smaller quantities of content, then focus on the material before considering more. Besides, many teachers allow regular online discussion attendance. The dialogue not only helps students learn new ideas; in some cases, grade points are awarded for daily participation in the class. Grades will fail in many ways if students log in only once a week or maybe twice.

Chapter 2: Advantages and Drawbacks of Online Learning

Learning and education are considered a natural part of working and personal life. It should not be ignored both for achieving a job and for acquiring knowledge. The online world is continually evolving, and this provides a great learning opportunity. Discovering how to learn with all available communication channels and to select the ones that best match a person's filtering style of knowledge is very critical.

Online learning today is becoming more and more popular. Many mainstream universities started free, sharing of their courses online. It represents an easy and straightforward method for attaining knowledge in nearly every area, including law and accounting, human sciences, such as psychology and sociology or history. Online learning is an excellent alternative to traditional universities, especially for people who can't afford to take regular courses with the time and resources available to them. But what are the benefits and inconveniences of studying online?

2.1 Advantages of Remote Learning

1. Comfort: Online students should arrange their study time around their schedule. They will work when they have the most time, whether it is early in the morning or late in the evening. Students don't have to drive to campus, so they can save time and research anywhere they want. Sometimes, they don't have to make it into the library because the course materials are always available online, and they save more time. Students can also learn at their speed and research as quickly as they wish. Of these reasons, online education is the ideal choice of students wanting to balance their obligations to work and family. The most significant benefit of an online course is that you (theoretically) have your classroom and teacher available 24 hours a day, seven days a week. Isn't going online your only reason for missing the class? Otherwise, everything is there for you. You can get updates, access notes, review assignments, take quizzes for practice, answer questions, talk with fellow students, and study whenever you wish. Other than the various due dates, you set your timetable to complete the course requirements.

2. Flexibility: You may study whenever you wish. You can study with anyone you want to. Online courses allow you the freedom to spend time with work, family, and friends, significant others, or some other activity you want. You can study wearing whatever you like (or nothing if you prefer!). You will have to complete the job (and this flexibility can be your downfall). But for many people, online study options cannot be beaten. These people may be the ones who continually shift work schedules, or people making usual business trips. Parents with kids, students caring for others, or whose health keeps them from getting to the campus regularly and the students whose friends or boyfriend/girlfriend drop in unexpectedly, also fall in the said category.

3. Less expensive: Online programs are typically cheaper than traditional schools. Students also save on the related training costs. For example, students taking online classes do not have the costs of commuting or campus accommodation. They are also possibly not required to buy materials for the course, such as textbooks, which are freely accessible online. Some courses online are offered at no charge. For any computer that's linked to the internet, users will know. There is no need to rent a house or pay for high maintenance bills to provide a learning environment for the students. Furthermore, students and teachers are no longer going to drive to college, thereby saving them money too!

4. Diverse Courses & Programs: Online career colleges offer students several options. Students can find the online classes they need or degree programs – from nursing to neuroscience. They can also receive online every academic degree. As online learning trends upwards, more colleges offer students an option to take online degrees. Ashford University, for example, an accredited online university, provides diplomas in many disciplines, including business management, social and criminal law, early age learning, and studies of human behavior.

University Rivalry means that you are getting greater rewards. Online learning is rising, even as university enrolments continue to decline. Translation: Universities work very hard to draw students towards their courses online. Universities are finding that online degrees will bring students from far. Consequently, there is a lot of rivalry between universities in which you want to get enrolled!

Hence, there is a more fabulous option of universities for the students. You are not only restricted to the universities in the towns that surround you. You will be able to choose from a large number of colleges. For universities from Britain, Australia, Canada, and New Zealand, you have the choice of any university that offers online degrees across your country. For American universities, you'll probably want to take advantage of government-based scholarships to go to a university in the state you're living in. Degrees online are evolving in leaps and boundaries. If you're signing up for an online degree, you're signing up for a kind, of course, that has a lot of money being poured into it by colleges fighting to earn the title of 'best online provider.' Universities will work very hard to keep you in their courses in exchange for your money.

5. Career Advancement: Online courses and degree programs, while seeking academic qualifications, encourage students to work. When working, taking online courses shows employers that you want to remain updated and can tackle new challenges. Penn State graduate, Kelsie Abduljawad, is a perfect example of someone who served while attaining an online degree. She earned a master's degree in leadership education, which she completed online via the Penn State World Campus. She worked at an all-girls Islamic school in Doha, Qatar, while she was receiving her degree.

You'll have experience using online learning resources such as Google Docs, Canvas, Blackboard, Webinars, Community Wikis, and Forums when you graduate with an online degree. To graduate with an online degree means you are a future-oriented, technologically competent employee of the 21st Century. You'll have a point of sale that the students on campus are less likely to make. This digital skillset would be at the forefront of your work application and could just get you on the shortlist to get hired on the interview day.

6. Greater Individual Attention: Since you have a direct pipeline via e-mail to the professor, you can have your questions answered directly. For fear of feeling stupid, many students aren't comfortable asking questions in class. The internet (hopefully) removes the anxiety (as long as the teacher feels comfortable). You sometimes worry about a problem after class, or when you're studying. Instead of trying to remember to inquire or forget about it, you should give the professor an e-mail. Your opportunity to know is heightened.

Following reasons depict why e-learning can be perfect for the introverts:

- **E-learning does not involve the physical presence of a student**: The online world is a place where introverts can stand alone yet together. In such an environment, when learning will happen, introverts can rejoice. The thing about being around people has everything to do with enthusiasm. Extroverts get energized in a crowd, while introverts drain their energy. Most people do not know this is happening, but it does. In an online learning environment, both teachers and students are not in the same space as the student. It means that the introverted student will not waste their precious time paying attention to what's happening with other students in the class but instead will concentrate only on the lesson.

- **E-learning is more self-paced:** Everybody learns differently, and every student advances in their way. But conventional teaching cannot consider this fact. All students will step forward at the same pace. Some who are going ahead need to wait for the others to catch up. Others who are struggling will have to deal with their learning gaps. Yet that isn't the case for e-learning anymore. Each student can grasp the concept at his or her own pace. Anyone who understands the learning materials can quickly finish the course in a fraction of the time. Those that need more time and additional clarification will get them to the same position without leaving anyone else stuck. For introverts, this lack of peer pressure is a great feeling.

- **E-learning means more writing and less speaking:** Having an oral presentation is an essential mastering ability; no one can argue about it. Around the same time, though, this is not the only form of evaluation. Too many people talk a lot and still say nothing. Students also need to know that every word counts. Most of the classroom exercises include more talk and less writing, but the other way around is for e-learning. By default, introverted students like to write more than talk. When you're writing, every word has more time to process. And most of all, before you share it with others, you can edit your comments— strip out any unnecessary words or add more for clarification.

· **E-learning offers more authority to the introverts:** Introverts are solitary creatures. Not only that, but they tend to figure things out on their own first — even the things that are harder to get — and they will only ask a friend or instructor for support when they meet a serious obstacle. They prefer the individual tasks of learning over group work. Because e-learning eliminates others' physical presence, introverted students can learn their way. Both the collaborative tools that a school LMS offers are fantastic to be available (and they'll use them!), but it's even better for these students to decide when to use them.

· **E-learning should go hand in hand with gamification:** The learning process never gets harmed by limited competition. But while most people compete with each other, the introverts compete with themselves. No matter how you look at it, it feels incredible to make noticeable improvements, and finally to win. As gamification elements can be incorporated so easily in online courses, competitive students will become more interested in what they study. Everybody's going to want to earn as many points as possible, add badges to their profile or get on the leader board. For introverted students, the most critical aspect of gamification may be the progress score.

7. It is modern: Today, most people tend to use the internet to access the content. Now, we're using the internet to read the news, watch our favorite television shows, and talk with friends, book appointments, shop, and more. Despite all the ease that the internet has brought to our everyday lives, why should education remain exclusively conventional rather than use the advantages that the internet offers?

8. Meeting Interesting People: Many of us, particularly in large classes, don't take the time to get to know our fellow students. Perhaps we're too distracted, or just plain shy. An online course provides the ability to get to know other students through newsletters, chat rooms, and mailing lists. Even if you're just chatting online, it offers you some kind of contact with other students and people that's just not realistic in the time-limited classroom on campus.

No technical innovation in man's history has connected the world with people like the internet. There is still a considerable variation between those who have Internet access and those who don't. The very fact that all of us can interact across the globe speaks about the value of this medium.

Several times in a course, the websites you visit are located in another country.

Can there be a better way to find out about Michelangelo's works than to go to Italy (of course virtually)? What better way can there be to learn about the Amazon rainforest or China's past or the customs of South Pacific islanders than visiting those places online? And if you engage in global learning days or other online activities, you can also catch up with someone in another country and make friends with them. After all, it is a small planet!

9. Self-Discipline: Procrastination is perhaps the greatest opponent of online courses. Some of the students, even teachers, put off the things which need to be done right up to the very last moment. If it comes to school, the last moment to know is the worst time possible. Often in the form of bad results at an exam or assignment, the lesson is learned the hard way. Yet, in the end, you are okay because you know the value of doing stuff on time or even in advance. That self-realization is what propels your online course success. No one is over your shoulder, waiting to tell you to go online and research. There is nobody there to get you to ask questions or post answers. You come with the ability to research in an online course. It is something student-centric or productive learning. The online student assumes responsibility for their study course and matures to become an adult for whom learning and achievement are highly valued. In short, that depends on you for your performance!

10. Promotes world skills and life-long learning: Understanding how to access knowledge online opens up a variety of chances for your personal and professional life. You can find online jobs, get online college applications, make online travel plans, and get online car dealer prices. You can also compare online shops, access great online works of art and literature, meet online people from around the world, follow online sports and movies, and so on! There are practically infinite possibilities. It gives you a definite advantage over someone who lacks those skills.

Usually, much of what we know in a course is forgotten at the end of the classes within a week or two. Finding that spark of curiosity and understanding how to find information online means you still have at your fingertips what your learning is. When you are interested in a specific subject, maybe because of something you see, read or hear about, or perhaps because you have a question from one of your kids or friends, you can get online and search it out. You will have developed the skills for finding information, digesting it, synthesizing it, and formulating an answer to any query that comes your way.

2.2 Limitations of Online Classrooms

Is there any limitation? Yes, online education does have certain drawbacks.

1. Excellent Time Management Skills Required: Believe it or not, online classes would take more time learning and completing assignments than an on-campus course does. How could this be? The education online is text-based. You will write notes, post comments, and otherwise communicate using your fingers (i.e., by typing) to connect with your teacher and other students. Typing is, as you probably infer, slower than talking. (Try to read each word as you type it, and compare the difference if you've spoken the same thing.) In the same way, reading the lecture materials can take longer than listening to the teacher delivering them, even if the lectures you've spoken have a distinct disadvantage. If you sit in a classroom, you will miss a large percentage of what the professor says, no matter how focused you are. For brief periods it is human nature to zone out. You may tend to go back through the notes as you're reading if you forget anything, and it takes more time. The point is you'll probably learn more in an online world, but you'll have to make a more significant effort to achieve that learning, and hence the time required for that.

An Internet-based course allows you to develop your time-management versatility. As in other words, if you don't utilize your time correctly, you will, of course, find yourself buried under a seemingly unconquerable coursework mountain. For completion of the studies, online courses require the self-control to allocate the time to study. This implies that learning online should be a priority, and one must not allow other things to intrude. Often, that means making tough choices.

2. Procrastination: Just as there is a dark side to that notorious property known as the Power, the Internet-based courses have a dark side too. This dark side starts with procrastination. Procrastination in an online course will rip you into parts. Nobody asks you to reach college on time.

Nobody tells you that assignments are due, or that tests are coming. No one may preach to you, continue with you, and plead with you to keep on top of your coursework. (Sounds pretty sweet, huh?) Learning and assignments can be easily put off in the online world. Weeks have gone before you know it, you haven't done any homework, and it is exam time already. Timid. Anxious. Creepy. All too true.

It is a strategy for a sink or swim situation, and you cannot get it both ways. If you want to become this planet's responsible, self-sufficient, independently minded person, then now is the time to start. Life is not a rehearsal dress. Get into it!

3. Isolation: No-one will hear you scream in an online course. And this, for some online students, creates discomfort. It can be frightening to research alone with only the machine as your companion. There's no whispering in the back of the school, no wise peanut gallery comments, no imposing voice at the front of the classroom, begging everyone to listen. The online world is a very different atmosphere. Some people need to get used to it.

Your online teacher will hopefully be receptive to this issue and will help you resolve those feelings. In any case, if they begin to hinder your studies, you should be aware of them and seek support. A fast e-mail to a friend, your professor, or counselor will make you feel better connected if you're lacking the sense of community you're looking for.

Since the students taking online courses cannot communicate with professors and other students face-to-face, communication is by online chat groups or e-mails. Developing relationships with classmates in self-running classes is especially tricky. New schools, on the other hand, have a campus to socialize with other students or study with them. You may also pause to ask questions or get input from a professor's office.

4. Own Responsibility: It's just you who are responsible for knowing. No one can put that on you or get you to read. Teachers can only share some information and experience, give you a couple of tools, and hope you'll get it. You must have the spark and the drive to fulfill your dreams. So, the only downside of an Internet-based course, in a rational way, is that you do not own it. You may not be taking control of your research and your goals. You might well get a long way behind and never catch up. Online programs offer more flexibility for students, which can be challenging for students who don't know how to deal with it. Online courses often don't have teachers hurling you to remain on track, which means students are responsible for their learning and may not own it. It's easy to slip back and not feel inspired to catch on. There are no resources in the online classroom to help students learn so that the learning process can become more difficult. In the end, students need to be self-motivated to advance promptly through their courses and programs.

5. The problem for instructors: Online education is also a bit of a challenge for instructors. As tech progresses, teachers are continually trying to keep up. Traditional professors believe in lectures, so handouts and transition to the online course program can be difficult.

6. Technology Costs and Scheduling: The most critical elements of online courses are software programs and internet access. Students may need to learn new skills in programming and troubleshooting, which may take time. Students may also need to purchase new software to access their online classes or pay extra for upgrading to high-speed internet. Another drawback is that students need to change their schedules according to the due dates of assignments, which could be troublesome for international students or others who don't live in the same time zone as the teachers.

In the same way, if your laptop fails as a student on campus, you might need to get help from the campus library to complete your essays. As an online student, if your laptop crashes, you can't even finish your weekly tasks. You are in trouble. Problems with technology can emerge during your online degree. Be ready. Have you got a friend where you can use your laptop? Does your instructor record your live lectures so you can access them later? And, of course, are you confident learning how to use simple online tools such as Google Docs and Canvas, or management systems for learning Blackboard? You don't need to know how to use them right now, but you need the courage to learn in the short-term future how to use these devices.

7. Communication Breakdowns: Often, you'll give your instructor an e-mail and wait, and wait, and wait for a reply. Three days pass, and you eventually get a response that is, at best ambiguous.

So, you're e-mailing back, demanding clarity. Another three days pass, and you're getting another comment you just don't quite understand. Quickly, a week has gone by, and you're still trapped in the dark. That is the truth for a lot of teachers and students who aren't most updated with technology. Thankfully, this should only happen with your online degree once or twice. The downside of online degrees is that when it comes to technology, the teachers are generally very switched-on. But even a well-connected teacher could misunderstand the tone of your e-mail. Likewise, you could struggle with their language. The truth is, there is no contact form just as good as face-to-face contact.

8. The College Experience is missing: When you're an 18 – 24 teenager considering going to university, what are the key reasons you're going to study? Do you like to join clubs, make friends and go out to parties? Do you want to use the university to meet your potential spouse and to make connections for future jobs? Going to university is a great social experience. A degree that is entirely online does not give you any of the social coherence. Therefore, online degrees usually attract alternative students. They attract students who are of mature age, who work full time, or who have their own well-established family and social life and thus do not need or want the 'college experience.' You need to ask yourself whether you still wish to enjoy the university experience or whether your focus is to study versatility when continuing with your current life studying online.

9. Group Work can be challenging: Many university degrees nowadays impose group research as a prerequisite to passing the degree. The ability to work in teams is a preparation capability for the workplace that employer organizations believe is ingrained into a degree. When it comes to studying online, you are not other than needing to do group work.

Dreaded are the community of students who study online. The fact that they're interacting with somebody they have never met physically scares them. So they're reliant on their partners to log in continually. The trick with online community work is to try and locate a partner who will regularly and early in the week post on the forums. If you're working with one of those dedicated learners, you're going to do well.

10. Plagiarism and Cheating: Keeping in mind that students use a computer and are not always being monitored, they may plagiarize essays and other assignments. Along similar lines, cheating in online tests can be easier for students. Online cheating is easier to do (and more difficult to detect). Although it's not clear if online students are potentially cheating more than face-to-face students, the fact is that it's not easier to track who is taking a test and how they do it online than in a classroom. Nevertheless, the universities and professors on the opposite end may adopt some tactics to help counter the issue. Using technology for the detection of plagiarism, for instance. Having students run their essays through a plagiarism for-fee detection service will theoretically discourage piracy on cut-and-paste. At the very least, it could start a discussion about how to cite sources correctly.

Although e-learning comes with some drawbacks, the fact that the advantages far outweigh the disadvantages cannot be denied. You will develop self-discipline, and it is an attribute that can help learners in ways that go far beyond schooling.

In conventional learning settings, plagiarism and cheating may also occur, and there are ways to avoid that from happening in online tests that cannot be found in a typical classroom. Isolation can be overcome by integrating various learning approaches as in blended learning, which fosters further student interaction. Online education is an excellent by-product of the modern age. It gives thousands of individuals, who otherwise would never be able to pursue their studies for any reason, the ability to complete a study course. It is now totally up to the human race how it brings it into its most effective use-curse or a blessing.

Chapter 3: Getting Started with Google Classroom

Google has partnered with educators to create a classroom: a simplified, easy-to-use resource that helps teachers navigate the coursework. The educators will build classes with this Classroom platform, allocate tasks, rate and submit reviews, and see all in one place. Google Classroom is a straightforward, easy-to-use program, but you can learn a lot of best practices along the way. Join the Revolution in Google Classroom! It will completely change how you deliver assignments, communicate, and collaborate in your classroom and give your students skills that are ready for the future! Google Classroom saves you time and helps you to communicate with your students. Start today with resources, tips, and tricks from such educators like you. Set up your classroom for success, and be prepared to be amazed at the ease and simplicity that Google Classroom brings to your workflow.

3.1 Introduction to Google Classroom

What is Google Classroom?

Google Classroom is free of charge web service made by Google for schools. It clarifies paperless structure, dissemination, and marking of homework. Google Classroom's underlying goal is to streamline the file-sharing process between teachers and students. Google Classroom incorporates Google Drive for the production and delivery of tasks, Google Docs, Sheets and Slides for writing, Gmail for collaboration, and Google Calendar for scheduling.

Students can be invited via a special code to enter a college, or imported automatically from a school domain. Every class creates a separate folder in the Drive of the respective individual, where the student can send work for a teacher to assess. IOS applications, which are available for IOS and Android devices, allow users to take images and add to assignments, share files from other phones, and offline access. Teachers can track each student's progress, and teachers can return work along with the feedback after grading.

But what distinguishes Google Classroom from the standard Google Drive experience is the interface between teacher and student, developed by Google for the way teachers and students think and work.

Evolution of Google Classroom

Google Classroom was revealed on 6 May 2014, with a preview available to individual members of Google's G Suite for Education program. It was launched publicly on 12 August 2014. By October 2015, Google reported that certain 10 million students and teachers were using it. Google said about 50 million students and teachers worldwide used Google software, from Gmail to Chrome.

In 2015, Google introduced a Classroom API and a website sharing button allowing school administrators and developers to continue their interaction with Google Classroom. In 2015, Google also incorporated Google Calendar into the Classroom for planned assignment dates, field trips, and class speakers.

In 2017, Google enabled Classroom to allow any personal Google users to enter classes without the need for having G Suite or Education account. And it became possible for any individual Google student to build and teach a course in April of the same year.

In 2018, Google announced a refresh classroom, introducing a classroom section, enhancing the grading interface, allowing teachers to reuse classroom work from other classes, and adding features to organize content by topic. In 2019, Google released 78 new illustrations of the classroom.

For the previous two years, Google has been taking its popular apps and equipping them for classroom use. Although many schools and districts tend to use traditional learning management systems, such as Blackboard, Canvas, Moodle, and Schoology, the eyes of teachers are gradually focusing on Google's Classroom Platform. Most schools are also using the collaboration software suite of Google — Docs, Sheets, and Slides. What Classroom seeks to offer is a way of bringing together these applications and applying new functionality to what teachers and students need. In short, the Classroom is aiming to be a lightweight framework for learning management.

According to the product manager at Google, they spent about a year and a half studying and talking to educators about the app. Apps alert from the guardians and the introduction of multiple teachers to a class were created merely from user feedback.

Does Google Classroom become an LMS?

Technically, it doesn't. Google Classroom is not a stand-alone program for learning management (LMS), course management (CMS), or student information (SIS) program. That said, Google adds new functions to Google Classroom periodically. For example, in June 2019, Google announced that schools would soon be in a position to synchronize the new grading features of the tool with an existing student information system. As Google continues to add features, it is likely to start looking, becoming more like an LMS, to work. Perhaps it's better, for now, to think of the device as a one-stop-shop for class organizing.

Is Google Classroom free of cost?

The Google for Education platform is free for schools. Still, there is a paid G Platform Enterprise tier for education, which includes additional features such as advanced video conferencing apps, advanced security, and premium support. Google no longer publishes information about pricing, so you'll want to contact them directly for a quote. Google also offers several free items for authoring tools, web themes, and professional growth, such as Chromebooks, and partners with other companies.

Implementation and integration

Google provides educators and IT Administrators with a range of training choices. These are:

- The Teacher Hub, which provides primary or advanced self-paced Google Classroom preparation and instructor professional development resources
- Train the Trainer course for people into teaching others
- Google software Certified Educator and Certified Instructor programs
- G Suite Certified Administrator program for IT administrators

Who is eligible for Google Classrooms?

· The classroom is open to:

· Schools that use G Suite for Education

· Organizations that use G Suite for non-profits

· Individuals over the age of 13 with personal Google accounts. Age can vary according to region.

· Both Domains in the G Suite

Google Classrooms Support Service

Users can access Google Classroom help in the following ways:

· The Help Centre offers information on different topics related to Google Classroom. There is also a troubleshooting section with solutions to common issues.

· There is a software community where users can seek advice from other Google Classroom users and Google Classroom staff.

· Google Classroom also offers regular updates with new features and other software enhancements.

· IT guides for schools' IT administrators also exist.

Can the Classroom be used if G Suite for Education domain includes Gmail disabled?

Yes. Gmail doesn't have to be enabled to utilize the Classroom. If your administrator has not activated Gmail, however, teachers and students do not receive e-mail notifications.

Note: If you set up your mail server and receive information from Drive, you can receive notifications from the Classroom too.

Could the Classroom be used if G Suite for Education domain has been disabled?

No. Classroom collaborates with Drive, Docs, and other tools offered by G Suite for Education to help teachers build and collect assignments, and students submit work online. If you disable Drive: Docs and other services are also disabled. You are not able to add these resources to the research that you allocate to students. Students would also not be able to add these to their jobs. The classroom can still be used, but the collection of features is minimal.

Difference between Google Classroom and Google Assignment

Google Assignments is for organizations using a learning management system (LMS) that want better grading workflows and assignments. It can be utilized as a stand-alone tool and a complement to the LMS, or it can be implemented into the LMS as an interoperability learning tool (LTI) by the school admin. If you are using the Classroom, you already enjoy the best of tasks, including reports on originality.

Accessing Google Classroom from school account and personal account

Most of the time, the classroom is the same for all users. However, since users of school accounts have access to G Suite for Education, they get further attributes, such as email summaries of student work for guardians and full user account management. G Suite for charity users has the same features as users of G Suite for Education.

Google Classroom for visually impaired people

Google Classroom is a resource designed to help teachers and students interact in the paperless classroom and remain organized there. Visual disability and blindness students can use a screen-reader to access and handle classes and assignments.

Following is the availability for various screen readers:

Web: With any modern browser such as Chrome, Mozilla Firefox, Microsoft, Internet Explorer, or Apple Safari, you may navigate the Classroom using a screen-reader. See the guide on how to set it up in your browser. You can use ChromeVox, for example, with your Chromebook. On Macs, the built-in screen reader, VoiceOver, is used.

Mobile

Android: The smartphone app for the Classroom works with TalkBack, a pre-installed screen reader that uses spoken input for interaction.

IOS: The Virtual Classroom app operates on IOS with VoiceOver. For specifics, you might need to see your device's accessibility settings.

Google Classroom API outline

The Classroom API can be used by schools and technology companies to create applications that communicate with Classroom and G Suite for Education and to make Classroom function better to suit their needs. The Classroom API is an API created by Google. That means non-Google companies will benefit from the resources and infrastructure that Google provides.

To use the Classroom API, developers must adhere to the Terms of Service of the Classroom API. Many programs cannot use Classroom data for marketing purposes. Third-party developers and administrators may use the Classroom API. Teachers and students must approve third-party apps. Utilizing the Classroom API, you can do many of the things that teachers and students can do programmatically through the Classroom UI. For example, you can synchronize with the student information systems, display all the classes taught in an area, and control the coursework.

Non-Google services can use the Classroom API to incorporate Classroom features. For example, an app may allow a teacher to copy and reuse a Google Classroom class, rather than re-create the level and re-add every student. Applications may also display, build, and change Classroom work programmatically, add materials to work, turn students' work in, and return grades to the Classroom.

The software must request authorization from the Classroom user before software or service can access Classroom data. The app asks for the individual permissions it requires (such as a username, email address, or photo profile), and the user may approve or reject the request made by the service. The Classroom API uses a popular Internet standard named OAuth to authorize access.

As an administrator of the G Suite for Education, you monitor how the data is exchanged within a domain. You can decide which teachers and students in your area can allow services to access their Classroom data in the Google Admin Console. By organizational unit, you can customize the access. You can also monitor the services that have been given access to a user's account in your jurisdiction in the Admin console, and you may revoke permissions if required.

The different tasks that the Classroom API can accomplish depend on what position a user has in a class. A user can be a student, instructor, or administrator just as in the Classroom UI. Teachers and students should accept applications from third parties and report misconduct.

When the consumer is a (n):

Student: The API can view the course information and teachers for that course.

Teacher: The API can build, display, or remove their classes, show, attach, or remove students and additional teachers from their classes, as well as view and return research, build assignments and topics, and set grades in their classes.

Administrator: The Classroom API can organize, view, or delete any class in their G Suite for Education domain. It can attach or delete students and teachers in their area in all the classes. It also looks at the work and topics in all of the classes in their domain.

There are many explanations for why Google Classrooms are being used for more and more classrooms. The technology is being implemented all around the world, including the US schools and districts through the 1:1 laptop initiative. The initiative features a learning laptop for every pupil. Chromebooks are often chosen because of their affordability and intuitive interface. They are easily integrated with the complete suite of Google apps that includes the Classroom.

The basic requirements to get started with the Google Classroom application are to get a device or gadget that would render the installation of application possible. Such devices may include a smartphone, tablet, laptop, or even a desktop. This would then be followed by access to a useful quality internet with fast speed and more MBs. Users would need to ensure that there are no power-cuts or any other issues which might interrupt the operation of their Google Classroom. It is, however, to be noted that Google Classroom application would only work in those geographical locations which have the internet services available. Furthermore, Google Classrooms provide course accessibility in various languages used in different corners around the world. These languages can be changed by adjusting the settings inside the application. A more detailed guide regarding Google Classrooms would be provided in the forthcoming topics of this book.

3.2 Features of Google Classroom

As the classroom is increasingly paperless, teachers need to start seeking strategies for handing out tasks, handling their classrooms, engaging with students, etc. An increasingly growing number of teachers find their way into Google

Classroom. An innovative immersive classroom with less emphasis on software and more emphasis on teaching. You needn't be a trained tech to manage this classroom.

Wouldn't it be awesome if you could arrange your students' tasks, resources, and grades in a single location? Thankfully, Google listened to the teacher's needs attentively for EDU and planned Google Classroom to do that. It can be defined as the anti-LMS since it is both easy and efficient. Students have a common source of information for assignments, parents can see missed assignments and progress for the students, and educators can handle digital assignments and communication more easily.

Google Classroom allows teaching to be more effective and meaningful by providing educators with a forum for student assignments, fostering collaboration among students, and promoting communication. Educators can create classes, distribute tasks, submit input from individuals, and see all in one place. The classroom also integrates easily with other Google resources such as Calendar, Google Docs, Photos, Drive, and others.

And the most relevant issue is undoubtedly this. How should you use the Classroom on Google? What's for you in it? It's completely safe, first of all. You're not going to need to upgrade to a pro edition, which will save you some money. Sure, $0.00. Nothing. You can get started after you have configured your classroom. Here's a rundown of what the prominent features of this wonderful application are.

Add announcements and lesson material: Offer advertising about your lesson to your students. The announcements include the lesson supplies. Such announcements will appear in the Google Classroom stream of your students. This way, the students will easily find anything.

You can attach materials from a Google drive, connect to that lesson in Google Classroom, add files and pictures from your phone, add a YouTube video, or add any other connection that your students want to see. That is so simple!

Add assignments: You can add an assignment to your course just as you add an announcement. It operates the same way except you get the option of adding a due date and rating it here. When they have to make an assignment, it will alert the students, and it will also appear in their calendar.

Marking or grading an assignment: You can then review and rate the assignments the students have sent in. There's room for feedback via a comment from a teacher. Instead, return the task to your students. The "Points" tab houses a grade book of the assignments and grades of the students.

Manage students: The students must, of course, be able to share their thoughts. Or don't they? That is entirely up to you! You can manage permissions, allow students to post and comment, comment only, or give the teacher the ability to post and comment only. Even the students can be e-mailed individually.

Post Questions: You can post questions to your classroom and allow students to have discussions by answering each other's responses (or not, depending on the setting you choose). For instance, you might post a video and have students solve a query regarding it, or pin an article and ask them to write a response paragraph.

Reuse the Assignments: If you reuse your curricula year after year – or at least reuse papers, you may want an update. You can now recreate assignments, announcements, or questions from any of your classes — or from any class, you co-teach, be it from last year or last week. If you pick what you would like to copy, you will also be able to make changes before publishing or assigning them.

Better Compatibility of Calendars: Users prefer improvements that boost workflow. The classroom will automatically create a calendar in Google Calendar for each of your classes over the next month. All tasks that have a due date will be added to your class calendar automatically and kept up to date. You can display your calendar from within the Classroom or on Google Calendar, where you can add class activities such as field trips or guest speakers manually.

Bump a post: Sticking posts have long been a feature on forums, tweets, or Facebook updates. Now you can also do it on Google Classroom by pushing every post upwards.

Optional Project-based learning due dates: Self-directed learning? If you're using long-term projects or other tasks with no due date, you can now build tasks in Google Classroom without due dates.

Add a Google Form to a post: If you're a fan of Google Forms (here's a post about creating a self-graded exam using Google Forms), this is a movie you'll appreciate. A lot of teachers have used Google Forms as a simple way to allocate the class a study, quiz, or survey. Teachers and students will be able to add Google Forms from Drive to posts and assignments and get a connection in the Classroom to see the answers quickly.

YouTube Features: Love YouTube, but is it about inappropriate content? Google listens. As it also includes content that an organization or school does not find suitable, Google Classrooms introduced advanced YouTube settings as an Additional Feature last month for all Google Apps domains. These settings enable Apps admins to limit the viewable

YouTube videos for signed-in users, as well as users who are signed-out on admin-managed networks.

Google has announced several changes to its Chromebook Device Platform. The app shop built for educators offers not only learning and development applications but a multitude of "ideas" to help motivate instructors to make the most of the technology in their classrooms. The latest customization to the Chromebook App Hub will make it even easier for teachers and administrators to use the latest Chrome OS hardware that students are using.

Drag and Drop: On the Classwork Page, Google rolled out the new Classwork page last fall, where teachers could stay organized and chart their classes. Nevertheless, teachers organize their classes in various ways and require more versatility in their resources in the classroom. So now, you can drag and drop whole topics and individual items in the Classwork, easily rearranging them on the list. On the Classwork tab, you can drag a whole subject to a specific location, or drag individual items into — and in between — themes. This feature was launched on mobile last year, and now it's time for it to hit the web.

Refreshed Ux: Starting in January 2019, users were also able to see that the Classroom had a better and new look and feel, first on the web, and soon on the mobile apps in the classroom. The Company launched Google's latest content theme back in 2014 to provide greater consistency across Google's products and platforms. You'll see a more fluid style flow among the changes — plus a new approach to form, color, iconography, and typography on both the web and the mobile app. This also makes the class code easier to access and project so that students can find and enter easily.

And finally, 78 new themes were launched with design illustrations, ranging from history to math to hairdressing to photography. Now, more than ever, you can customize your Classroom.

Improved Training & Help: The need for more help comes with new resources and improvements. In the Teacher Centre, you could find the revised videos with the latest template and functionality that were rolled out in 2018 on the First Day of Classroom Training. New and enhanced Help Centre was created while Google support was at it, in tandem with the Group and product platform.

So what is new?

With tablets, convertibles, and touch-enabled devices increasingly trending in the classroom, new specifications in the Chromebook App Hub will let teachers find apps designed for these form-factors quickly. Here are some examples from The Keyword:

- Search for your favorite apps and ideas and share them with other educators.
- new filter options that enable teachers to search for the best app to improve their Chromebook tablet lessons by topic
- software feature and Google integration, and the ability to filter apps through privacy laws such as GDPR and COPPA

The last filter has allowed more than 20 applications to be updated already to take advantage of Chrome OS tablet mode, which will support users such as the newest Chromebook tablet Lenovo 10e.

Below is a detailed outline of all the updated features Google has introduced so far, over the last few years.

April 2020

New feature: Video class meetings—Teachers can start for distance learning, and students can enter video meetings in Classroom with Google Meet.

Only teachers in the Classroom can build video-meetings. Both video meetings produced in the Classroom are called nicknamed meetings, so if the teacher is the last person to quit, students cannot start a session before the teacher, or enter the meeting. These permissions will vary according to how the school administrator sets up Meet.

To use Meet in the Classroom: School accounts must be used by teachers and students and be in the same domain. Admins have Google Meet to turn on. Admins can find further support for distance learning in Set up Meet.

Additionally, the new G Suite Enterprise for Education capabilities will be available free of charge to all Classroom educators using G Suite for Education by September 30th, 2020. Such apps include live streaming, recording, and video meetings for a class of 250 students. Live sessions are available on the Classroom's Web and Mobile versions.

January 2020

New features: Notifications of originality — Teachers can now turn on three assignments per class for originality results. The reports highlight source material for students in their research and flag missing references so they can improve their writing. Teachers will display reports after the students send work to check academic integrity and provide input from the grading tool. With G Suite Enterprise for Education, administrators can upgrade to unlimited originality reports.

Rubrics — Teachers can now build rubrics and reuse them. After the completion of work, students could review the rubric of an assignment to help them stay on track. As teachers rate rubrics, level choices will automatically determine a cumulative grade, which can also be manually modified. Students will quickly check their rubric feedback upon returning to work.

All about rubrics: Customizable—up to 50 requirements and ten-value standards Shareable—Import and export options when you build interchangeable assignments—**Reuse a rubric in another assignment Note:** Rubrics roll-out course by course, and should be available in a few days.

New mobile features: See overall grades—if teachers share whole categories, students can see the overall grades on a mobile device (Android and iOS).

See rubrics — on a mobile device (Android and iOS), teachers and students can see the rubric of a task.

New beta programs: School matches — Expands originality reports inside the school to check for events. For information, go to Sign up for Beta programs in the Classroom.

Internationalization — Reports of originality appear in multiple languages. For info, go to Sign up for Beta programs in the Classroom.

August 2019

The new smartphone features: Show beta rubrics — Teachers and students can now see rubrics on their Android device or IOS.

Enhanced IOS app — Students would press "Your job" to show their files at an assignment.

New updates: Classroom with the Classwork page- Google launched a new Classroom edition with additional functionality in August 2018, including a Classwork page to help teachers coordinate classwork. Teachers may also return to the previous Classroom edition.

The last version (without the Classwork page) was deprecated on September 4, 2019, and discontinued. As a result, teachers were no longer able to have the option of deleting the Classwork page or reverting to the previous edition as of September 4, 2019. Any classes that were using the previous version were migrated automatically to the new version beginning September 4, 2019.

For teachers, what does that mean?

Any classes they had in the previous version were migrated automatically to the current version beginning September 4, 2019. Class resources were not transferred to the transformed courses in the Class Settings tab. Such materials (excluding YouTube content) could still be accessed in the teachers' Drive tab. By adding the same stuff to the Classwork list, they could create a similar experience

If you, the teachers, were using the previous Classroom version, you were enabled to move it to the new version by adding the Classwork page before September 4.

What would admins do?

Although instructors were informed of this change through in-product notifications beginning in August, Google recommended notifying instructors of this update in the domain.

New features for August 2019: Beta originality reports—you can now sign up for beta originality reports. Teachers should turn on stories of originality while they are making an assignment. For more stuff, go to Sign up for Beta programs in the Classroom.

June 2019

New features: Archive a class — Teachers are now able to archive mobile device classes on IOS.

Redesigned student assignment page—Students are more likely to apply research and communicate with their teachers than ever before. Go to Request an Assignment for details.

Gradebook: The Grades page—Teachers will record grades from the Grades page and return them.

Grading systems — Teachers can select one grading system for each class.

Grade Categories — Teachers may assign classwork posts to grade categories.

Overall grade — if an instructor wants, students will see a class for their overall score.

Docs grading tool — Teachers may receive input from the Docs grading tool and grant grades.

New Beta programs: Link grades to your SIS — Teachers can transfer classes to their student information system (SIS) directly from the Classroom. To voice interest, administrators can go to the sign-up page for beta interest.

Rubrics — Teachers can build and save custom rubrics for assignments to grade and share feedback with students. Teachers or administrators can go to the Beta sign-up page for rubrics to show interest.

May 2019

New apps for Android: New tablet grading view—Teachers can apply grades on tablets to a list of submissions on the left, and give the individual student feedback on the right.

The Preferences tab has a fresh look.

New IOS feature: Student Selector — Teachers can randomly select students to use the Student Selector to call.

Randomly pick a student: This information is mainly for teachers. Teachers can use the Student Selector of Classroom to call on their pupils randomly. The student selector selects students randomly from the class roster. Teachers could call a student, skip a student to call later on, or mark an absent student. This functionality is only available on mobile devices running Android and IOS.

Note: The Student Selection is neither accessible nor visible to the students.

The following steps might help:

To select a student

· On your mobile app, pick a student and tap Classroom icon, then Classroom, then your class, and then People.

· Tap Student selector icon, then Student in the top-right corner

· **Choose one:** Name the student shown and then tap "Next" for another student.

· You can switch to the next student on iOS devices too.

· Tap Call Later, to skip the student display.

· Tap Absent to identify the shown student not present for the selection session.

· (Optional) Tap Start Again at the end of the meeting if you wish to reset.

To see the class roster

· To see a list of those who were marked as Selected, Not Chosen, or Missing, go to the roster.

· Tap Classroom icon, then Classroom on your mobile app, later on, your class and then on People

· tap Student selector Student icon, then selector in the top-right corner

· Tap Not Selected, Picked, or Absent under their numbers.

· You'll see which students haven't been chosen, picked, or absent.

· To get back to the Student list, tap Open Back or Close option in the top-left corner.

Reset the student selector

- Click on the Classroom icon, then Classroom on your mobile device and later on your class and then on Students.
- Tap Student selector option and then selector in the top-right corner
- Tap Reset, in the top-right corner
- Tap Reset to check again.
- All students are indicated as Not Selected.

April 2019

New features April 2019: New work now posts to the top of the Classwork list.

Teachers will filter the Classwork page by theme now.

New features for Android: Co-teachers can now leave a class on the People's list.

An instructor can be inviting you to teach as a co-teacher in their class. Once they enter a class, co-teachers will perform all of the instructor's tasks. Primary teachers and co-teachers, however, in Classroom have separate permissions.

Such essential distinctions are:

· The primary teacher can only delete a class.

· The principal teacher is unable to unwind or be excluded from the course.

· Teachers are not permitted to be silenced in a class.

· The primary teacher manages the Google Drive class folder. The co-teacher is granted access to the class Drive folder after a co-teacher enters the class.

· Your G Suite administrator could just encourage your school teachers to begin classes. If you have trouble adding yourself to a class, please contact your admin to change the class membership settings for your domain.

· If you quit a class that you co-teach, you cannot open it again unless you are re-invited or enrolled in the class as a student.

Accepting an invitation

· Head to classroom.google.com to approve a request, and press Sign in.

· Log in to your Google Account. For instance, you@yourschule.edu or you@gmail.com.

· Select Allow on the class card if you want to teach the lesson. If not, please press Decline.

· **Note:** If you're a college member, it does not delete you from college by clicking Decline.

· (Optional) The invitation can be accepted by clicking on the link in the invitation document.

Leaving a class

You have two ways to quit a class as a co-teacher.

From the list Classes:

· Go to classroom.google.com and then press Sign In.

· Sign in to your Google Profile. You@yourschool.edu, for instance, or you@gmail.com.

· Click the "More" option and then Leave Class on the page you want to quit.

· Tap "The Leave Class" option to confirm.

From the People page:

· Select More and then Leave Class across from your name.

· Click on Leave Class to confirm.

Share files with the primary teacher before leaving a class. The primary teacher will access all the data you have generated in the class in the class Drive folder. You can link them to the class Drive folder if you want to share other files, such as notes or an attendance sheet. The data or directories you add to the class Drive folder can only be accessed by teachers and co-teachers. When you share them, students cannot access the files or directories.

· Go to the.google.com classroom, and press Sign In.

· Sign in to your Google Profile. For instance, you@yourschool.edu or you@gmail.com.

· Select the Open folder on the class card.

· Click New in the top-left corner and then select an option: Folder — to add a new folder for your files to the class Drive.

- Import file — to access a folder that was developed beforehand.

- Upload of the folder — to delete a folder that was generated before.

March 2019

New features: Improvements to private comment

notifications — Private comment notifications can now be switched on or off. You will also obtain them separately from other updates about the job. By default, you get email alerts for a range of things, such as when someone comments on your post or returns work to your instructor. These notification settings can be changed at any time.

Students and teachers are permitted to:

· Turn on or off all alerts.

· Select what updates you'll get.

· Turn on or off alerts for class.

· Turn on or off email alerts.

You can deactivate all alerts from the Classroom.

· Go to the.google.com classroom, and press Sign In.

· Sign in to your Google Account. For instance, you@yourschule.edu or you@gmail.com.

· Select Menu, at the end

· Click the Settings button. (You will need to scroll down)

· Next to Receive email alerts, pick one: To turn off alerts, click "Off." To turn on notifications, click "On."

Customize alerts

You can choose which updates you are getting for all grades. You can, for example, turn off invitation notifications for all classes, but leave notifications of assignments on.

· Go to the.google.com classroom, and press Sign In.

· Sign in to your Google Profile. For instance, you@yourschule.edu or you@gmail.com.

· Tap "Options" at the top of "List." (You may need to scroll down.)

· (Optional) Press the "On" button next to "Receiving email updates."

· Tap on any notification to turn it on or off.

For a summary of each form of notification, see the list below.

Notifications from teachers

To learn when to:	Turn on:
Someone comments on your article	Comments on your articles
Someone mentions you in an article	Comments referring you
A student sends you a private email	Private feedback on work
A student resubmits work	Student Work submissions
An instructor invites you to teach a course as a co-teacher	Invitations to co-teach classes
A planned post that was published or failed to post	Scheduled post

Student Notifications
To learn when: **Switch on:**

To learn when:	Switch on:
Someone replies on your post	Comments on your post
You are tagged in a post or comment	Comments that mention you
A teacher sends you a private comment	Private remarks on the job
A teacher makes a task, request, or an announcement	Work and other posts from teachers.
A teacher grades or returns work	Returned work and grades from your teacher
You are invited to a new class	Invitations to join classes as a student
Your work is not submitted that was due within 24 hours	Due to date reminders for your work
	published or missed

Switch off class alerts

You can choose whether to receive updates for a specific class or not. For example, if you don't want any notifications for your Math class, you can turn them off, but for your other classes, you will still get notifications.

Note: When alerts for a class are switched off, all signals for that class are switched off.

· Go to the.google.com classroom, and press Sign In.

· Sign in to your Google Account. For instance, you@yourschule.edu or you@gmail.com.

· Tap Options at the top of the List option. (You might need to scroll down.)

· (Optional) Click the "On" button next to "Receiving email notifications."

· Click Down arrow next to "Class Updates."

· Click the" On" or "Off "icon next to the class name

February 2019

New features

Stream notifications — if you're using the Classwork tab, select a compressed or extended view on the stream for Classwork notifications, with the option of entirely hiding them.

Flow organization — in classes that use Classwork, transfer each post to the top of the line.

Class details include necessary information, such as the class name, section and room number, Settings for posts on your stream page, your class video meeting link, and your class code. You can change class details on your Settings page.

January 2019

New features:

New look — unique style and lots of new themes.

Drag-and-drop classwork — Organize whole subjects or individual posts easily on the Classwork board.

Show and exchange a class code quickly — Class codes for each class are now at the top of the Stream tab.

Swipe for options — rapidly removes or edit posts by swiping left on your smartphone (IOS only) device.

You need to know some things before you continue using Google Classroom for the wrong reasons. It's an online learning site, but it's not:

A chatbox: You can reply to assignments and ads, but no chat feature is available. You can give them an email if you want to be in direct contact with your students, or you can allow other Google apps to take over this feature. Dream of Meet Hangouts!

A test or a quiz tool: When it comes to making quizzes in Google Classroom, there are several possibilities, but it's still not supposed to be a quiz tool. In that end, there are so many other good games. Think of quizzes about Google Forms.

Option 1: You can add assessments and assignments inside Google Classroom from other educational applications, such as an automatically graded test from some good platform.

Option 2: Inside Google Classroom itself, here's what you can do: add a question. Then select a clear answer or an item of multiple choice. It does not sound all that impressive. If you want to enhance communication in your digital classroom interactive, it's best to choose the first choice.

Discussion forum: Announcements can be made, and students can vote on them, but it's not a perfect place to talk. Check out some other featured applications if you're looking for a natural but powerful, free classroom resource that will inspire discussions (and other cool things).

Some insights into the Originality Reports and other features

Google Classroom features that are now accessible to all users were previously only available in beta. Originality Reports and Rubrics are among them.

Originality reports

The originality reports of Google Classroom act as a resource for correcting uncited content and possible plagiarism. This functionality is no longer in beta mode – it is now available in English for everyone who uses Classroom (Spanish, French, and Portuguese are in beta). To make this function applicable to an assignment, the teachers simply have to tick the box.

At present, teachers can turn on originality reports for three tasks free of charge (if the school uses G Suite Enterprise, then there are no limitations). Both teachers and students can conduct the reports at any point during the assignment. The reports include expiry dates (since web material changes continuously). Teachers will use the tool up to 3 times before the students return their homework. Teachers are allowed to access reports for each submitted paper.

If the originality report has been completed, the link to the 'view originality report' will open the story, where any problems are highlighted. The report shows the flagged content context and emphasizes the commonalities in bold. Clicking on the passage will take you straight to the questionable content website. Eventually, there will also be school-owned content repositories within each domain to test the work of the students internally. There is a toggle choice between seeing the total percentage of the flagged assignment and the number of flagged passes. The method is less about "catching" a student in misconduct, and more so about allowing them to recognize and fix possible misunderstandings before finalizing their research.

Citations using Explore

Students can use the Explore tool to cite sources that would enable students to insert footnotes in different citation formats. They simply click on the button and Explore finds connections between the topics of the documents and the content online. The paragraph in the chosen form (e.g., APA, MLA, and Chicago) is referenced by clicking on the quotation mark icon next to the correct document. Once the resource is quoted, it appears like this in a footnote: when reporting, it is expected that there is no flagged material, but this does not guarantee a plagiarism-free paper. And when passages are quoted, when an originality report is produced, the reference(s) must show up. Teachers will also use their judgment to assess if there has been plagiarism.

Rubrics

Although some briefing on rubrics has been done in the features mentioned above, it shall be discussed in some more details here. When submitting an assignment, the Rubrics feature allows students to see the grading requirements, which can help teachers grade more effectively.

The rubrics may have several parameters and point values. As of now, a numerical value must be added to each point. The details for each criterion will be shown or hidden by clicking the arrows on the right (next to the point total).

Assignment rubrics can be generated by starting from scratch or importing the requirements into a Google Sheets format. Note the time-saving tricks of duplicating criterion when constructing a rubric (click the 3-dot 'more' menu) and, of course, copying and pasting! Scoring is optional; the scores will be automatically added to the grade book in the 'Grades' or 'Marks' tab if the teachers want to rate the students' work.

Teachers may reuse a rubric from a previous assignment, or even from a different class. Open the job to be graded when you use a rubric to grade work, and press the grading button below the files button. Here you can, if appropriate, adjust the overall score and input scores for the different parameters. You may also provide private feedback for each student, just as with other assignments. Rubrics can provide timely, personalized, descriptive feedback on work for students!

Google Forms-a complementary tool with Google Classroom

Google forms are among the most valuable tools of Google Drive and are, without a doubt, one of the most reliable devices on the Internet. If you need a contact form or a checkout page, a survey, or a directory for students, away is all you need to collect the information quickly. It only takes a few minutes, with Google Forms, to make one free. Google Forms — along with Files, Cards, and Slides — is part of Google's tool kit of online applications that help you get more accomplished in your browser for free. It's fast to use and one of the easiest ways to directly transfer data to a spreadsheet, and it's the closest sidekick to the spreadsheets of Google Sheets.

Teachers may use Google forms to obtain information about the students. These forms can also be used as a sample before taking an exam. Once the students get the right question, they proceed to the next question. So if they get the question wrong, it will lead them to a support page to discuss the subject and then return to the issue to try again. Teachers will use this to collect knowledge on how they're doing for their big exams and quizzes. With several graded questions, they may build multiple-choice, short responses, essay questions, and much more. Since teachers use technology in their classrooms and often adopt the flipped model, they need to know if the students can access the internet at home and how confident they are with using technology.

It would be smart to ask their students some questions about what sort of technology they are using, how secure their internet connection is at home, how comfortable they are with using technology and what technology they are using. If the teachers have this knowledge, they will use it to help the group students and make sure they have someone good with it who will support them. They should also make sure the students who do not have the internet at home have a place to watch the videos that have been flipped.

Google Forms began life as a feature of Google Sheets in 2008, two years after the initial launch of the Sheets. A spreadsheet may be attached to a file, converted into a separate sheet, and displayed in another layer with your answers. It was necessary, but the job was done. Over time, Google added more features to the Forms, and eventually converted it into its standalone app in early 2016. Today at docs.google.com/forms, you can create and manage forms with templates and easy access to all of your ways in one place.

Google Forms is now a full-featured form application that comes to your Google account free of charge. In any sequence you want, you can add standard question styles, drag-and-drop questions, customize the form with simple picture or color themes, and gather answers in Forms or save them to a Google Sheets tablet.

The easiest way to start creating a form is via the Google Forms app. Go to docs.google.com/forms, either pick a template or open a new type. Within Docs, Sheets, and Slides, there is also a link to Google Forms: press File-> New – > Form to start a new empty form. Or, press Tools-> Create a Form in Google Sheets to start a fresh, unique style that is automatically connected to that spreadsheet. This is the easiest way to get data into a new or current spreadsheet: open the worksheet where you want the content, start a form, and the answers to the form will be saved there automatically without any extra clicks.

The editor for the Forms is straight forward. Your form fills the screen center with space for a title and definition, followed by fields for the way. To edit it, select a form field, and add a question. Use the drop-down box next to the question to pick the form of a problem, such as multiple-choice, checkboxes, short answer, etc.

Google Forms provides various settings. The floating toolbar to the right helps you to add more fields to the form. You can change the color scheme of the arrangement in the top-right menu, display the way, and use the Submit button to upload the form and access other extra choices, including the installation of Forms add-ons. To see current responses to your question, switch from the Questions tab to the Responses tab in your Question Editor and add it to a List.

Google Forms contains 12 types of fields: 9 types of questions, including text, picture, and video. To add a new question, just click the + icon in the right sidebar or click on the text, image, or video icons to attach media to your form. For a simple way to add questions that are similar to your style, each field includes a Copy button to duplicate the track. There's also a delete button, options to render the appropriate area, and a menu on the right side with extra choices. You can switch the question types at any time, although note that if you transfer from multiple choice, checkbox, or menu to other question types, your field settings and questions will reset. Then, to quickly fill in field questions, just click enter to start adding another one.

Title and Description: Title and description fields are automatically added to each form and field — although the description is hidden in most areas by default — and you can use the **Tt** button to add an extra block of titles anywhere. For questions, you can leave the title and summary blank, but you have to fill in the primary type of text.

The definition does not include formatting options — although you can include links (in a condensed format, such as links.com, or as the full-length style such as https:/links.com/), and readers of the form will click those to access the site or related content.

Short Answer: This area is the best place to request tiny bits of text: names, email addresses, values, etc. To answer the question, you get one line of text — although, your users may potentially enter as much text as they wish. This area involves data validations for number, text, duration, and standard expression to ensure you get the answers you need. Number validations help you search for value ranges, while text validations are ideal for email addresses or connections to check for.

Paragraph: This is a field for text — long-form text is almost the same as the short answer field. The only data validations available here are duration and regular expression, so just use it when you want thorough input or longer notes in the answer.

Multiple Choice: The default area in a Google Form for new questions, multiple choices allow you to list options and let users select one. You can then either make the form switch to another section, based on the answer or shuffle the response options to avoid bias.

Checkboxes: Similar to multiple options, this field lists answers and allows users to select as many as they wish. It also requires validation of the data to allow users to pick a certain number of choices. This does not, however, contain segment hops.

Dropdown: Do you want all the answers in a menu? For you, this field is here then. It's the same as the area of multiple-choice — with the same segment jumping and shuffling options — only this time, the answers are in a line. It is useful if you want to keep your form compact because there are several choices to address.

Linear Scale: The area enabling people to pick a number in a linear range, allows you to set a scale from 0 or 1 to 2-10 with the lowest and highest choices labels. And yes, emoji do function for labels as well.

Multiple Option Grid: This could be the most confusing field because the fields are shown in a list rather than in the matrix when the readers see them. Essentially, you are going to add questions as rows and column choices. As many rows and columns can be created as you want, but remember that readers will have to swipe right to see more than six columns on desktop browsers or only three mobile columns. While setting up grid queries, you may want to keep the form preview open — just tap the eye icon at the top right, and refresh that page to see your changes. The grid also allows you to require a response per row, in addition to the standard response option, and can also limit users to only one response per column.

Date: Want to ask for a particular date or period, maybe scheduling an event or logging in an activity? The date field is the one you wish to pick. It may request a date and month as well as, optionally, the year and period. Remember that the date format will be shown to your position in the default format. If your Google Account is tuned to US English locale, the dates will be displayed as MM / DD / YYYY, while UK English accounts will display dates as DD / MM / YYYYY. Your users can see the date choices in the date format of your locale unless they are entered into your Google Account, so be sure to keep that in mind when designing the forms.

Time: Time allows you to request a period in hours, minutes, and (optionally) seconds to log precisely how long it took an operation.

Image: Google Forms allows you to upload a photo, insert a photo from a connection or Google Drive, or take a picture from your webcam (as long as Flash is installed). Or, Google Photos can be searched for images, including royalty-free stock pictures and Life photos that are allowed to be used inside Google Drive.

Video: Google Forms support YouTube videos only, which you can find by searching or by connecting to a link.

If you have incorporated photos or videos, your entry form will be compatible with the standard title and description, along with options for resizing and displaying the video or picture-oriented, left, or right.

Form Sections and Reasoning

Simple communication forms require only a few fields, but longer surveys on one page can easily get daunting with hundreds of questions. That's where sections come in handy: to answer one set of questions at a time, they let you break up your form into parts. Just click on the right toolbar at the last button to add a section below the current issue. Every section contains its title and definition, as well as an arrow button at the top to view or hide questions and to keep your form editor clean.

Although you can drag-and-drop questions between lines, you cannot rearrange full lines. Instead, you might push out the questions and then delete the line. And, if you wish to repeat a segment, simply click on the menu of the segment and pick Duplicate section for another copy of those queries. That's the perfect way to start a logic-jumping form. Say you'd like to ask a respondent follow-up questions based on their answers — maybe ask which meat a participant needs, but only if they're not vegetarian.

Simply add sections with the optional questions, then either add a section jump to the multiple selections, checkbox, or menu questions, or the section itself. Make sure you think about where people who shouldn't see these questions are also sent, maybe in a different section with alternative questions. Or, if there is nothing else to ask, you can give them straight up to the end of the form to request their responses.

Be creative: Form sections and jumps allow you to turn your form into a mini-app, and they can be a great way for each person to condense comprehensive surveys into only the most relevant questions.

Create a Quiz

Another way to do an interactive form is via the Quiz feature of Google Forms. You can find a tab of Quizzes within your settings for the form. Select Make this a questionnaire, and then select whether to show the results immediately after submission of the form or later after reviewing the answers. If you choose the latter, the form will demand that respondents sign in with their Google account. If you choose, you can then choose to display the missing and right answers, as well as a value for each choice. You can see a new Response Key button at the bottom left of each question, with this activated. Tap on it, then pick the right answer to the question. Optionally, you can provide comment reviews for both correct and incorrect responses, with a link for respondents to see more details if you wish.

Plan Your Form

There's one place where you have no option: your form's design. Google forms include a color or image header, and a lighter color accent as the background. New forms come in purple by default, while the prototype shapes also have an image. To tweak your style, press the color palette icon at the top-right if only a little. You can choose from 15 colors with a complimentary background hue, each one a darker color to the header.

To pick a photo or Google Doodle-style drawing from Google's library, click the photo icon as the header photo of your page. Or, pick one of your Google Drive photographs or upload a new one and crop it to fit in as a header for the form. Forms will then automatically pick a color matching your picture history.

Some of the header photos used are animated GIFs featuring burning candles, rolling balls, and more. Sadly they appear as a regular still image if you add them to your form. Google Forms may be getting support for GIF in the future — for now, icons and colors are the only design choices in Forms.

Store Form Responses in a Spreadsheet

Once the form has been generated, you do not need to do anything extra to store answers from the respondents in

Google Forms. By default, it will save any answer in the Responses tab, showing overview graphs and answer lists. A view of an individual response shows the live form along with each respondent's results. That's great for quick form responses, but you can connect your form to a Google Sheets spreadsheet for more tools to analyze answers. Just click in the Responses tab on the green Sheet icon or press. Select Answer Destination in the menu, then create a new spreadsheet or pick an existing one to store the answers.

One great thing about saving entries from Google Forms to a spreadsheet on Google Sheets is that it's easy. Change the field names of your form, and they will be changed automatically in your table document. Get a new entry, and as soon as your recipient clicks Submit, it will appear in the list.

Google Forms still maintains a complete copy of all data about your form, so don't worry if you accidentally delete anything from your spreadsheet. Just open the answer settings for your Form and unlink it from your spreadsheet, or press Form-> Unlink Form within your spreadsheet. Then reattach the form to your spreadsheet, and Google Forms will restore all the data from the form to a new file.

Share completed forms online

Ready to receive responses? Select the Send button to share the form via email or social networks in the top right corner, copy a connection to the form, or get an embed code to add it to your site. You can either copy a full-length link with the link or get a shortened goo.gl/forms/link to share on social networks more easily. The embed choice provides options for the width and height to suit the shape within the context of your web. Sharing the form via e-mail requires an additional option: sharing the e-mail form. This copies into the email your actual form choices, and if your user uses Gmail, they can fill in the form in their Gmail inbox, press Send, and send in their reply without ever seeing your original form. It only works in Gmail, though — Apple Mail displays the fields of the form but doesn't submit the answers to Google Forms, and Outlook.com can't even open the form — so you may want to attach a notice to non-Gmail users with the request.

Share Paper or PDF Form

Need to collect offline responses? Here too, Google Forms will help. Just press Print in your Form tab, and a ballot-style copy of your form will be made by Google Forms that you can print or save as PDF.

Grids and multiple-choice options display pill buttons to fill in, while text fields contain clear answers. Simply type your answers into your Google Sheets spreadsheet to save them along with your other entries in the form until the respondents have filled out your paper forms.

The teachers when operating the online classrooms frequently use the Google Forms. The quizzes, assignments, and other tests created using these forms would help ensure the effectiveness of Google Classrooms.

How is Google Classroom supportive of classroom differentiation?

Google Classroom may help streamline the formative assessment, which is essential to help students who may need more support or additional questions. For instance, you can use the platform to build, distribute, and collect digital exit tickets or auto-graded appraisals quickly. Google Classroom can, in a way, make it easier and faster to gather daily feedback on the progress of your students. There are, of course, plenty of other formative evaluation resources out there, many of which now provide Google Classroom integrations.

Google Classroom also makes it easy for individual students or small groups to customize assignments. This means teachers will give other students or classes in a class changed or different tasks. You also have the option to check-in privately with a student to see if they have questions or need some extra help. The ability to do all of this online may make the distinction efforts of teachers less visible for the class, something that could be beneficial to students who might feel singled out. Differentiation will always be a matter of creative problem-solving with or without a tool like Google Classroom, and there is no one or "right" way to do that. Fortunately, many teachers post online their ideas, strategies, and innovative solutions.

3.3 Simple steps for setting up Google Classrooms

Google Classroom's simple setup method is relatively straightforward, even for first-time users. The Google Teacher Centre offers multiple tutorials to get started — if you are looking for the most popular videos and details, this is your best bet. There are also plenty of do-it-yourself tutorials shared by professors and software development experts on YouTube. Some of these videos produced by teachers provide practical tips and techniques they have learned in their classrooms by using the site. Okay, so, now that you've come this far, that means Google Classroom has to say something to you! You would find it easy to set up and very intuitive to continue to use it. Follow these steps to set up your teacher account at Google Classroom:

Step# 1: Signing Up

Since we speak to students about using Google Classroom, it is presumed that you are in a school or district that uses G Suite for Education. It's also believed you know your Google login information that your school or IT department has given to you. Finally, it is thought that you must log into the Classroom from a laptop or device connected to the internet. Before trying it on a smartphone or tablet, it is recommended to do so. You can use the Classroom by logging in with a G suite e-mail address when you go to classroom.google.com, or you can use it for educational purposes without claiming to do so. This way, it works just fine too. If you have hundreds of pupils in your class, it's just harder to manage your students. You're going to have to add them one by one.

Step# 2: Set up a class

As a teacher, designing a class is one of the first things you'll do in the Classroom. In a class, students will be assigned work and get to have announcements posted by the teachers. If you are teaching multiple classes (at the secondary level), then for each section you are teaching, you would create one class.

Adopt the steps below to create your first class:

- Go to classroom.google.com and log in.
- Select the role of the teacher.
- Click the + icon on the home page of the Classroom and then pick Create class.
- Give the class a title that makes sense to you and your students.

The following are optional but might be relevant to your teaching situation:

· Click Section and enter the details to enter a short description of your class, grade level, or class time.

· Select Subject to add a subject such as Algebra I, and enter a name, or select one from the category that appears when you enter text.

- Click Room to enter the classroom venue and enter the info.
- Click on the Create button.

You can now see a class code shown, but that's not going to be necessary right away. When you can invite students to your class, you will come back to that at a later date. If you need to see the code at any time, you can display it on the Stream tab.

Congratulations, you now have your first Google Classroom created. You're well on your way to improving student learning by using Google Classroom.

Step# 3: Inviting students to the Google Classroom

Once you've built your class, you can invite your students to participate. Let them sign up by entering the unique code you've given them using the Google Classroom app. You can find the code in your class which was developed. Go to the "students" page. Another choice is to allow your students to enter their e-mail address, one by one. One thing you should keep in mind is that your students need an e-mail address from Gmail or Google.

You can also have your students visit classroom.google.com to let them in. You can select "join class" there, enter the class code, and your students are in! This could be a little faster as you don't have to type in the e-mail address of every student. Now get ready for your online lesson! At least, it's there, and it's accessible to everyone. You have to do a few other things before you can take off for good.

- **Make your first task, or an announcement:** You can share a new statement in the Stream, or go to Classwork- click on the "+ Create" button and share your first assignment to Google Classroom. Don't forget to have your tasks numbered. The students will find it easier to see which one comes first because you can't reorder tasks in the stream. You can also transfer tasks up to the top. Press the title to see if any students have handed in the assignments. Also, give grades and feedback later on. You will then return the tasks to your students so that they can start editing again.

- **Attach some lesson material to your curriculum/task:** Fill in Google Drive material or add a YouTube video, a computer file, a connection, etc. You will find those options right below the due date. If you just want to share your class presentation, which is not related to an assignment, you can go to the "About" tab. A few lesson materials like slides, interesting papers, and examples can be added here.

- **Open the folder on Drive:** Each time a new class is created, Google Classroom creates a Drive folder for that class. You can navigate the folder by going to all tiles in your lesson. You can find a folder icon on each piece of tile. Click on it, and you will be in the folder. You can add materials for the class here too. Most of your student assignments end up in the Google Drive folder automatically, and you'll get it back whenever you want.

3.4 Adding and Grading Assignments

Although this feature has already been highlighted to some extent in the discussions above, this section will bring in some in-depth info on adding and grading assignments using Google Classroom.

Making an assignment

Students just love homework, and as a teacher with Google Classroom, you can easily add assignments that include the attached content. After the assignment is posted, the students receive an e-mail notification of the task, after which they complete it and return it. The cool thing is that they lose edit rights for that assignment after the students turn in the assignment, which means they can't change it. Then, the task can be marked.

Here's how to make your class assignment:

1. Log in to your class and click on the Stream tab if it's not already displayed.

2. Select File.

3. Type in the assignment title and optional definition. The description is a perfect place to bring the task directions in.

4. If you need to, press the due date to change it.

5. Press "Add Time" to add the time of day when the assignment is due.

6. Click the correct icon:

· **Paperclip:** This option adds a file to the assignment if you have materials to add to the assignment. You can import the file from your hard drive here, which is saved in your Google Account.

· **Google Drive:** This option always adds a file to the task, but lets you locate the data right on your Google Drive.

· **YouTube play button:** This option allows you to add to the assignment a YouTube video. You can either check for the video on YouTube or copy or paste the YouTube video URL when you press this button. YouTube results are shown right in the same window while you are looking for a video, and you can even preview the video, so there is no need to visit the YouTube site.

· **Link:** You can press the chain-link button on the chain to paste the assignment in an external URL.

You can grant permissions for documents that you upload or select from Google Drive for what the students will do. To allow students to do the following, click the drop-down list:

·   **View only:** Select this option if you want all of your students to read the same data but don't want to change it. That is only good for materials of comparison.

·   **Edit:** If you want all of your students to make changes to the same file, choose this option. That is only good if students are supposed to work together on a single assignment.

·   **Make a copy for each student:** If you want each student to have their copy of the assignment, choose this option. Students will make adjustments and make different turns in the task. This is ideally applied to traditional homework assignments where the student is responsible for their job.

7. Click Assign.

The assignment is made, and every student is informed of the task by e-mail. The task appears on the Stream page of the class, on which you can check how many students have completed the task.

Although you can upload files created in non-Google applications, such as Microsoft Word, it is easier to use the forms of Google Drive to build documents if you are going to share them in this way. Google Files, Sheets, and so on are entirely incorporated into the Classroom, and when you complete your assignments, your students won't have to jump through the hoops. For instance, if you upload a Microsoft Word document, the student would have to download the document to complete it, re-upload it when it is finished, and add it to the assignment again. Or they would need to open the file in Google Docs to complete it and re-attach it to the assignment. It removes most of those steps by building the document in Google Docs, to begin with.

Learners and students will report on the assignment at the bottom of the assignment on the Stream tab. Here you can provide additional explanations, or students can give general feedback about the assignment or ask questions that all the other students will see.

Grading the assignment

With Google Classroom, the days of learners handing out papers and homework assignments are gone. As an instructor, you can make your assignments with any extra resources, such as handouts or worksheets, in your curriculum. Students complete and return the assignment-all electronically on Google Drive. You can also rate them online after your students turn back into their assignments. Here's how:

1. Sign in to your class and click on the Stream tab if it doesn't already show up. In the center column, you will see the assignments that you have made.
2. You can see how many students have completed the assignment in the Task box, and those who have not completed it. Click on the number above the "Done" option. You can then see the list of students handing in the task.
3. Select the student's name to extend his / her assignment.
4. Tap on the folder attached to the student's assignment to see what the student turned in. The document opens in the appropriate Mobile app (e.g., Mobile Docs).
5. Make any remarks inside the document that you have.

To stand out from the student's text, you should type your comments differently. Much as in the old days, when the teachers marked a homework assignment using red pens, you can use red text to add feedback. Or, better yet, the input can be received using the Comment feature. Simply highlight the text you are commenting on, and select Insert and then comment option. Type the comment in and press Comment. All of your comments are stored automatically in the document the student turned in.

1. Close the document to go back to the work page for the students.
2. Select where it says No Grade to grade the work.
3. Type the number of points awarded, between 0 and 100. In this area, letter grades are not recognized.
4. Check the box beside the assignment for the student.
5. Select "Return." Assignments have to be returned to the students before documenting them.
6. The classroom will ask you if you still want the assignment to be returned, and if you want any input. Upon completion, click Return Assignment.
7. The task shows in the assignment list as returned. The student receives an e-mail that you returned the assignment and, if necessary, can edit the assignment, and return it.

When making assignment worksheets, it's best to use the apps from Google Drive, such as Google Docs, Papers, etc. This is because the Classroom is wholly incorporated into Google applications. If you are using third-party programs, such as Microsoft Word, then you and your students need to download the files, re-upload the data, and re-attach them to the task. Using Google apps does away with all the hard work.

Pro time-saving tactics while grading assignments

Some teachers add a private message, for each student, in each task when grading in Google Classroom. And while on some tasks, each student needs unique comments, others allow the teachers to repeat comments.

The comment bank in the grading tool for Google Classroom is super helpful, but it is often found that only 3-4 clicks can often add up to insert a comment, mainly while working with several students. That leads to the invention of a pro tip for Google Classroom time-saving: submit a private message to multiple students at once. Here's the flow for this:

· Teachers, with the Classroom's grading tool, can go through the assignments of the students, one by one. If the student needs a specific comment, then they can grade, comment, and return from the assignment tool area the work of that student.

· Teachers can only enter their grade on the assignment tab, and no feedback, for the students who meet the criteria for an assignment.

· If the teachers have finished all the student work, and are returning all the assignments with specific feedback, they can go back to the Assignment Student Work page. This is the page where they can see all the tasks of the students in one location. There is a list of who's turned in, who's still missing, and who's been graded. It is here that the time-saving magic takes place!

· Select all of the turned-in assignments with a single click, and then hit "Return." At the bottom of this pop-up box is a private comment option. Type the positive feedback, then click Return, and Google repeats this private comment for every student and returns all assignments in one click!

Why not free up as much as you can to spend on what you love? In education, opening up an entire day, afternoon, or even an hour can be incredibly difficult. Professionals must be time scavengers, demanding minutes along the way, and those minutes will add up to hours if they are intentional.

3.5 Privacy Evaluation for Google Classroom

The terms of Google state that they use knowledge to help improve the services' protection and reliability. They state that they make contractual obligations in their agreement on the G Suite for Education and that they are committed to compliance with the privacy and security requirements.

Safety

Google uses knowledge to help improve the services' security and reliability. This involves identifying, preventing, and reacting to fraud, harassment, security threats, and technical issues that could affect Google, its users, or the public. A school will offer students access to Google resources like Google Docs., Sheets, Slides, and Sites. These aids allow students to interact in real-time with their peers and instructors, allowing them to share their work, gain feedback, and make edits instantly. They may be kept private, shared, or even made public, with others (such as a parent or the entire class. When users share information publicly, search engines, including Google, can index the information. The services offer different content sharing and deletion options for users.

Privacy

Privacy G Education Suite allows users to create a Google Account, which is developed and maintained for students and educators to be used by a school. The terms state the school may provide Google with some personal details about its students and educators when establishing this account. In most cases, it includes a user's name, email address, and password but may also include secondary email, telephone, and address if the school wishes to provide that details. Google may also specifically collect personal information from users of G Suite for Education accounts, such as telephone numbers, profile photographs, or other information that they attach to a G Suite for Education account.

Core features of the G Suite for Education include Gmail, Calendar, Classroom, Contacts, Drive, and Docs. Sheets, Slides, Sites, Talk / Hangouts, and Chrome Sync. Under its G Suite for Education agreement, these facilities are made available to a student. In addition to the Core Services, users of the G Suite for Education will have access to other Google services commonly accessible to customers, such as Google Maps, Blogger, and YouTube. Such concepts are considered "additional services" because they are beyond the core programs of the G Suite for Education.

For G Suite for Education users in primary and secondary schools (K-12), Google does not collect or use any personally identifiable user information (or any information relevant to a G Suite for Education Account) for advertising purposes. No data is taken to create advertisement profiles, whether in core services or other Google services accessed while using a G Suite for Education account. Parents and educators, however, should be aware that Google may serve advertisements in the "additional services" to G Suite for Education users. Still, administrators have the right to limit access to those additional services. Finally, the terms of Google state that they do not own any user data in the core services of the G Suite and do not distribute or sell G Suite data to third parties.

Security

Google Security terms state that they are entirely committed to the protection and privacy of user data and that they protect users and schools from attempts to misuse it. Google claims that its systems are among the most reliable in the industry, and oppose aggressively any unauthorized attempt to access data from customers. The terms of Google state that all facilities used to store and process user data comply with fair safety requirements that are no less stringent than those in facilities where Google stores and processes its similar type of information.

Google's terms further define that it has introduced industry-standard systems and procedures to ensure the protection and confidentiality of user data, to protect against potential threats or hazards to user data security or privacy, and to protect against unauthorized access to or use of user information.

Furthermore, Google's data centers are using new hardware that runs a new rugged operating system and file system. For protection and efficiency, every one of these systems has been optimized. The terms state that since Google manages the entire hardware stack, it can respond rapidly to any threats or vulnerabilities that might arise. Google's terms and conditions say that it must take reasonable steps to ensure that its staff, contractors, and sub-processors comply with all security requirements to the degree relevant to their scope of operation. These steps include ensuring that all individuals allowed to process personal data have committed to confidentiality or are subject to a reasonable statutory confidentiality requirement.

Google's terms also state that they encrypt Gmail and Google Drive data (including attachments). Additionally, user data uploaded or generated in G Suite services will be encrypted at rest. The terms state data are encrypted into multiple layers. Google forces HTTPS (Hypertext Transfer Protocol Secure) for all user-to-G Suite transmissions and uses Perfect Forward Secrecy (PFS) for all of its services. Google also encrypts message transmissions using 256-bit Transport Layer Protection (TLS) with other mail servers and uses 2048 RSA encryption keys for authentication and key exchange levels. This prevents the exchange of messages as users often use TLS to send and receive e-mails with third parties. PFS does not allow private keys for connection to be stored in permanent storage. Anyone who loses a single key will no longer decrypt connections worth months; also, HTTPS sessions are not retroactively decrypted even by the server operator.

Finally, if Google becomes aware of an unauthorized data infringement, the terms state Google would immediately and without further delay inform users of the data infringement, and immediately take appropriate action to mitigate harm and protect user data.

Compliance

Google's terms of service state that they make contractual obligations in their G Suite for Education arrangements and that they are committed to complying with privacy and security requirements. Whether it's real-time dashboards to check system performance, ongoing Google process auditing, or sharing Google's data center location, the terms state that Google is committed to providing full accountability to all its users.

The terms of G Suite for Education state that its core services comply with the Family Educational Rights and Privacy Act (FERPA). Where user data contains FERPA Education Information, Google will be deemed a "School Officer" (as defined in FERPA and its implementing regulations) and must comply with FERPA. Additionally, if schools allow users under the age of 13 to use G Suite for Education, Google's terms state that they contractually require schools to obtain parental consent using G Suite for Education as specified by COPPA.

Schools are also expected to obtain parental consent for the collection and use of personal information in the "additional items" that the school may choose to use with students before allowing any End User under the age of 18 to use these services.

In primary/secondary (K-12) schools, parents of G Suite for Education users may access their child's personal information, export the data or request that it be removed, via the school administrator. School administrators should have parental control, export, and deletion of personal information that is compatible with the services' functionality. The terms further state that if a parent wishes to avoid any further collection or usage of the child's details, the parent can request that the administrator use the service controls at their disposal to restrict the child's access to features or services, or remove the child's account entirely.

3.6 Apps for creating content for Google Classroom

Google Classroom coordinates with hundreds of educational programs. These integrations save time for teachers and students and make sharing knowledge between Google Classroom and their favorite apps seamless. Below is the list of some useful applications which work closely with Google Classroom to make learning an enjoyable experience.

Actively learning

This constructive learning application works smoothly with Google Classroom. Teachers can quickly synchronize Classroom rosters to actively learn and synchronize Actively learning assignments and grades back to Google Classroom.

Additio App

Additio App is a collaboration package that lets teachers stay organized and contact students and families efficiently. It provides other useful tools, such as a strong grade book and a durable lesson planner.

Aeries

Teachers can connect or build new classes based on their Aeries classes, and import scores into the Aeries grade book.

Aladdin

This integration enables the automatic development of Google Classroom classes based on classes in Aladdin. Assignments and grades between Aladdin and Classroom can also be synchronized.

Alma

This app is the first Student Information System to provide full integration with Google Classroom. Teachers can synchronize assignments and grades with this integration, and tech teams can deal with the creation and management of Google Classroom classes through their schools and districts.

American Museum of Natural History

The American Museum of Natural History provides Educational K-12 services and resources. To share related papers, curriculums, and tools, use the Share to Classroom option.

Aristotle Insight:K12

This all-in-one classroom management, content filtering, and monitoring system empower students to become informed, and safe digital citizens.

Assistants

Provides synchronous feedback to teachers and students when students complete assignments using this free online resource.

Book Widgets

Book Widgets provides collaborative workout models. To engage students, teachers can choose between over 40 different widgets or templates.

Brain POP

With Brain POP, teachers can import their classes directly into My Brain POP from Google Classroom. SSO-ready student accounts are created when a teacher imports a class, enabling students to log in to Brain POP through the Google launcher menu.

Buncee

A design and presentation platform to develop immersive educational material for students and educators allow learners of all ages to imagine ideas and connect creatively. Simply build your task, note, class reminder, activity, or project and share it in your Google Classroom with the students.

CK-12

CK-12 platform provides a library of free online textbooks, animations, quizzes, flashcards, and real-world applications for over 5000 topics ranging from arithmetics to history.

Classcraft

With the incorporation of Classcraft, teachers will take a single click to pull rosters from Google Classroom and provision accounts. Teachers could give timely turning in points to the students' assignments submitted well in time, in the game, and translate their Classroom results into points of the game.

CodeHS

CodeHS is a robust framework designed to help schools teach informatics. They have online instructor tools and resources, and professional development curriculum.

Curiosity.com

Their mission is to spark curiosity and encourage learners. This app develops and curates engaging topics each day for millions of lifelong learners around the world.

Nearpod

Nearpod is a presentation device. It is a lot more than that! Make your immersive introductions. Add some slides, slide by slide or select a particular Sway template that you can adjust. All of those slides make an excellent interactive presentation. Especially when you're introducing activities such as quizzes, open-ended questions, surveys, questions are drawing, and others. Inside your presentation, what about taking your students on a field trip? Only add a slide from Nearpod's library, featuring a virtual reality experience.

When your presentation is ready, your students can choose to enter a code in their Nearpod app or just click on the connection in Google Classroom assigned to them. You are in charge of the interpretation as an instructor. If you turn to another slide, the students' presentation on their devices will turn to that slide as well.

If your students have to do a quiz or questionnaire, they could do it on their computer, as it is part of the presentation-a live set of responses! So, you can see how your students responded immediately.

Duolingo

Is teaching a language a hard job to do, and a hard thing to understand for students? Duolingo is also one of the most popular Google Classroom applications to use! This app works well and is seen as the most popular language teaching and learning device in the world. Through the 23 languages it provides from Spanish to French, Russian, Dutch, Swedish, Italian, Hebrew, and more, your students can learn to be fluent in any language by continually practicing with this program.

Duolingo teaches a language through enjoyable lessons of a bite-size nature. It also helps you to record yourself talking and seeing what speaking in another language is like. Although Duo the owl keeps track of how well you're doing, you can practice talking to Bots in real terms! And yes, Duolingo is linked to Google Classroom, and it's one of the best applications to use for teachers.

Chapter 4: Google Classroom-An Interactive Platform

If you want to build a more connected platform for students, you might be considering doing so on the Stream page of Google Classroom. The Stream is a feed within Google Classroom where everybody in the class can find announcements and upcoming assignments, and it is the first thing students see when they log in.

Some teachers use the Stream to set up class discussion boards, where students can connect online by asking questions or commenting on the posts. Such discussion boards will help improve class engagement and give more leverage to students in getting their voices heard (or read) by the teacher. You can use the Stream as a closed social network of sorts with conversations, and it can be a great way to help children practice using all kinds of different digital citizenship skills in a "walled garden" style environment. Google promotes interaction in its classroom application to ensure a more significant outcome.

4.1 Engagement through student-teacher interaction

Once a student logs in to complete an assignment, they will make a class comment to which all other class-fellows and the teachers assigned to that class will receive a notification (through email and app notification) that students and teachers will reply to. This can be an enormous opportunity for both the teacher and students because they can answer a question or assist the whole class with a misunderstanding.

A student can also send a private message to the teacher if they want to ask a question without their classmates' prying eyes. After all, the same social problems are evident in the digital world as in the Classroom (How many times did you, as a teacher, have to deal with student social media conflicts?).

The following ways can bring in more significant student-teacher interaction with Google Classrooms.

With Google Classrooms, teachers can:

· Organize, distribute, and compile assignments, materials for the course, and student research online. Teachers are often able to post a task to different classes or to change and repeat assignments year after year. This would bring in some interaction between teachers and their students.

· Communicate about the classwork with the students. They can use the site to post announcements and notes about tasks, and it is easy to see who has finished their job or who has not. They may also check in privately with individual students, answer their questions and give support, as already mentioned in the beginning.

· Offer timely feedback to the students on their assignments and assessments. Google Forms can be used inside Google Classroom to build and exchange quizzes, which are automatically graded as students turn them in. Not only would the teachers spend less time grading, but their students will provide direct feedback on their work.

Engagement through videos

Educators can provide grades or reviews electronically without ever having to deal with paperwork by using open technology. Additionally, all work on the course is saved so that students can revisit it while they are at home. Students can also complete assignments via Google Classroom and communicate with teachers. This two-way communication method makes teaching and learning using the platform more convenient. By incorporating video, it makes engaging students even more comfortable.

Below are some reasons why videos could be helpful in a Google Classroom:

- **Video facilitates collaboration and learning:** In Google Classroom, multimedia is used by educators to improve the course work. Many are making videos within their class as interactive learning resources. By using video platforms, educators can create video tutorials or lessons, provide student input, use as assignments for students, or capture lectures all with a click of the record button.

- **Feasibility in access:** By using videos, educators can interact effectively and keep students learning without ever having to waste time in class. The videos are sent home and viewed in flipped or mixed learning scenarios. The student will learn from home, which makes them more interested in the Classroom.

The Classroom is an online application that can be used anywhere. Educators are given access to their videos on multiple devices with an account. They can quickly jump between devices and have access to video recordings.

With the Chromebook apps, educators and students both can record and share their videos. Videos can be stored directly on Google Drive. All files uploaded are stored in a folder in the Classroom. This makes videos easily accessible to teachers as well as students.

- **Saves Time:** Video is incredible for time-saving. Forget about typing out long assignments or grading documents! With video, educators can film assignments and be able to assign them all in a few minutes. The educators will add a video file with instructions when they make an assignment in a Classroom.

- **Encourages teamwork and communication:** Video encourages collaboration and strengthens conversations. Google Classroom gives students several ways to work together. Teachers can encourage online student-to-student discussions and create group projects within the tool. Students will hold talks with each other with video and complete tasks as assigned to them. Also, students can collaborate on Google Docs and share their work with teachers easily.

It is an immersive learning environment that is collaborative. By using videos, they can further enrich the experience. With Classroom, teachers can separate assignments, integrate videos and web pages into classes, and create shared group assignments for students.

- **Strengthens the student-teacher bond:** Video provides a more reliable link with the students. Positive feedback is needed for students to learn. This is a worthy aspect of all learning. So why not do it by video? Recent studies have shown that at a higher level, video mentoring and feedback requires students to communicate with teachers. It gives them a bond that they would otherwise not get in a group environment. Video offers a one-to-one friendship without being face to face.

Google Classroom educators can easily grade assignments. They can give any student personalized feedback. There's also the opportunity to comment on the grading tool. Additionally, the Classroom app in smartphones helps users to annotate research. Google Classroom can save all kinds of grades quickly.

Record the video, go to the screen recorder and press the 'record' button. You need to upload and publish the video when it is finished and provide the students with the link. They can access it from anywhere.

Film and share every instructional video with your students. You can monitor them while they watch the video lecture. You will be able to see if your pupils watched your video. You will also realize when the students started watching exactly, and to what section they kept coming again. Video analytics help you understand what interests or engages your students, which part of the video needs further detail, and where your students lose interest.

4.2 Engagement through student-student interaction

Originally, while using the class comment feature initially, teachers did find some sorts of distractions-there was all the usual chatter typical in social media design. However, once the students started using Google Classroom, the teachers began to note a slightly unexpected advantage of the class comment feature. Students began to answer each other's questions. In their online Google classrooms, not all classes or students do this, but the ones who do excel. While teachers need to step in and answer a few questions, students do teach one another for the most part!

The SRS (Student Response System) built into the platform is a prominent new feature. This helps teachers to inject questions into the stream page of the Classroom and start question-driven discussions with students answering each other's answers. Teachers may post a video, photo, or article, for example, and include a question that they want their students to answer. This way, teachers can learn and check in on the progress of their students, which is a fundamental practice. They can do that very quickly with this new functionality, from anywhere at any moment.

To increase interaction among online students, teachers can assign them group projects. Forcing students to work together will add new experiences for the students and contribute to strong collaboration among them. The most efficient way of learning is group learning. This offers students a chance to support their fellow mates and to learn to work together. Teachers should get the students together in small groups to prepare and let them and their team create a video project. They may ask them to take photos, record meetings, and upload and complete the project documents such as pictures or audio files.

However, if the students don't get along or their work styles aren't compatible, it can also backfire. Online, this dynamic can be exacerbated because students work with only a limited understanding of the personalities and activities of their fellow students.

4.3 Parental inclusion in Google Classroom

With the Google Classroom App, you can connect parents' email addresses to their kids, which helps parents to monitor their child's home learning closely. Parents, although, cannot see or engage with class feedback, they simply receive an email notification that their child has a home learning assignment, so it is important to have parental buy-in to ensure that students develop and accomplish as much as possible. Google refers to parents and families as "guardians" who may elect to receive summaries of unfinished assignments, upcoming assignments, and other class activity by email.

One way to ensure greater parental involvement in Google Classroom learning experience is to organize the evening meetings for the parents and teachers. Teachers and staff can use Google Classroom as a centralized place to book evening appointments for parent-teacher consultation. All instructors are included in Google Classroom, and they can consider the creation of an appointment sheet much as and when students are given an assignment. In such a form, teachers can book meeting dates with their students, and the school administration would immediately know when the appointment is. This might help make the whole evening coordinated much better and run smoother.

Chapter 5: Google Classrooms-Advantages and Limitations

The Google Classroom analysis below states some benefits and drawbacks to help you determine if Google Classroom is suitable for your e-learning courses.

5.1 Advantages of Google Classroom

1. Simple to use and easy to access from any device

Even if you're not a regular user of Google, using Google Classroom is one piece of cake. Aside from being provided via the Chrome browser, it can also be used from all laptops, cell phones, and tablets. Teachers may add as many learners as they want. They can create Google Documents to handle assignments and updates, upload YouTube videos, add links, or download files from Google Drive very easily. It will be equally simple for learners to log in, as well as to collect and turn in assignments.

2. Good connectivity and exchange

One of Google Classroom's most significant benefits is Google Docs. These documents are stored online and shared with an infinite number of people, and when you make an announcement or assignment using a Google Doc, your learners can access it directly through their Google Drive, as long as you share it with them. Besides, in Google Drive files, Google Docs are conveniently stored and customized. In other words, to exchange information, you no longer need emails; you just build a text, exchange it with as many learners as you want and voila!

3. The assignment cycle speeds up

How about making and distributing an assignment with just a click of a button? And how about learners turning in a matter of seconds their completed tasks? Making and turning in assignments has never been quicker and more effective, because you, as a teacher, can quickly check in Google Classroom who submitted their homework and who is still working on it, and give your feedback instantly.

4. Proper feedback

When it comes to feedback, Google Classroom allows you to offer your online support to your learners quickly. This ensures feedback becomes more prosperous as new reviews and remarks have a more significant impact on the minds of the learners. Google Classroom is a resource designed to help teaching and learning. It is an excellent interactive forum for the students along a course or level that the instructor can customize according to their teaching style and community profile and objectives. There are several ways for teachers to use the Classroom. In essence, it can be used in a teacher-led conventional way or used more creatively in a more contemporary manner, which in effect will lead to more innovation and collaboration among students. There is a diverse range of content available online — websites, classes, YouTube videos, forums, etc. — that provides tips, strategies, and creative ideas to help teachers use Classroom in creative and inventive ways to match their learner needs.

5. No paper required

There might be a day when it would be impossible to imagine grading papers; Google Classroom is undoubtedly keen to get there as soon as possible.

You have the opportunity to go paperless and avoid thinking about printing, distributing, or even losing the work of your learners by centralizing e-Learning materials in one cloud-based venue! Google Classroom allows students' access to resources, no matter where they are since everything is posted online. Students cannot lose their research in case they have physically lost it in their presence. Since they typically operate on Google Drive, everything is immediately saved, and excuses are dwindling. Students will encounter more organizational performance with a few short lessons about how to use these online resources properly. Hence, gone are the days of lost worksheets or rubrics. When required, absent students can easily access classroom resources from home – this will also help save teachers and their students a lot of stress in the long term.

6. Clean interface, and user-friendly

Google Classroom invites you while remaining loyal to clean Google layout standards, in an atmosphere where even minute detail about the design is simple, intuitive, and user-friendly. It goes undoubtedly with the saying that users at Google will feel right at home.

7. A good device to comment on

For a variety of online courses, the learners may comment on specific locations inside images. Teachers can also create URLs for new comments and use them for further discussion online. This has been shown frequently that technology engages the students. Google Classroom can help students get involved in the learning process and remain active. For example, if teachers have students answering questions in the Classroom, other students will comment on those answers and expand thought for both students.

8. It is for everyone

Educators can also enter Google Classroom as learners, which means Google Classroom can be set up for you and your co-teachers. You may use it for faculty meetings, exchanging knowledge, or professional development.

9. Language and competencies

When the teacher who produces the class or group of students shares content, teachers may take charge of the language levels and keep them related to their learner community, using language at all levels as appropriate. Teachers can slowly develop the learning environment and distribute the course materials at the speed of their classes, depending on the subject requirements and group profile. The choice of which students they are inviting to specific classes enables teachers to delegate work based on the particular learning needs of their students. Teachers can build classes of up to 1000 students and 20 teachers, allowing teaching by a team where appropriate.

10. Content of language learning

A handy feature of Google classroom is that once they've submitted it, it helps students to go through their work. Teachers will get updates about the students' reworks or feedback on something they find difficult. This ensures they can give the students who need it, individual attention, and give them more opportunities to show their learning, operating at the right speed for them. Teachers can easily discern knowledge by determining which students may need extra help, who might want to work with response grids of model responses, etc. The Google Translate plugin for the Classroom is also available to English language teachers.

11. Exposure to an online world

A lot of colleges today expect students to take at least one online class during their degree research. If one gets a Master's degree in education, some of their online coursework might be eligible. Sadly, many of the students never had any online education experience. That's why, at a young age, teachers really should make sure that their students have as much exposure to the online world as possible. Google Classroom is a simple way for students to assist with this change because it's super user-friendly, making it a perfect technology intro.

12. Differentiation

Google Classroom is an ideal resource for differentiation, as teachers can set up several different classrooms. If teachers focus on a topic in the Classroom and have groups that focus on two different levels, they can simply build two different classes for that subject. This means they can reach out to those who struggle with their kind of job without making them feel bad or dumb.

This can help teachers offer assignments on a more individual basis, and can also really reach out to some students. They can even break people into groups where teachers think they can work the best together. Google Classroom is a perfect, versatile way to make sure every student gets what they need, and as instructors see fit, they can quickly delete and recreate classes.

13. Saves time and cost

Students lose out on all of the 'hidden' costs of studying at an institution by taking online courses with Google Classroom. This includes travel costs (which in some cases are very high), the costs of printing out assignments, and so on, and the stationary and notebook costs.

Although it is difficult to determine how high these costs would be before the students enroll in a course, some important considerations should be pondered over. More specifically, how far a student would drive to an educational institution every day (and how much parking fees if they're commuting by car). If that turns out to be a significant number, they could save money by taking online courses.

Most students find that taking Google classes saves them a lot of time since they work from home-no time is spent on regular commuting. They can even take on a part-time job if they have any spare time, so they can earn while studying. This is perfect for those looking to maintain some kind of stable income while at the same time acquiring additional qualifications through Google Classroom.

5.2 Limitations of Google Classroom

1. Complex account management

Google Classroom doesn't enable multi-domain access. Also, you can't sign in to access your personal Gmail; you need to sign in to Google Apps for Education. As a consequence, if you already have your own Google ID, managing Google Accounts can be challenging. For example, if your Gmail contains a Google document or a picture and you want to share it in the Google Classroom, you need to save it separately on the hard drive of your device, log out, and then log in with your Google Classroom account again. Pretty much trouble.

2. Too much 'Googlish.'

Google users can get confused for the first time, as there are several buttons with icons that are only familiar to Google users.

Also, despite improved collaboration between Google and YouTube, which dramatically helps with video sharing, support for other standard tools is not built-in. You can find it annoying that you need to convert a primary Word document to a Google Doc to work with, for example. All in all, in the Google Classroom environment, you'll only find yourself relaxed as long as the resources you're using fit with Google services.

3. Problems editing

When you create an assignment and send it to the learners, the learners become the document's "owners" and are allowed to edit it. This means they can erase any part of the assignment they choose, which may create problems, even if unintentionally, it happens. Also, after you edit a post, students don't get a notification.

Also, there is no direct video recording option. It would be helpful to be able to quickly and directly record voice and video messages into the Classroom at Google. Users can record the videos outside the Classroom, and then upload them as an attachment.

4. Sharing work with learners

Learners are unable to share their work with their peers unless they become "owners" of a document, and even then, they will have to accept sharing options, which will create a rift if they want to share a document with their 50 + classmates say.

5. Limited integration

Google has restricted integration options and still needs to expand these options.

6. Updates are not automated

Event feed does not automatically update, so learners have to check and regularly refresh to avoid missing important announcements.

There are both advantages and limitations of Google Classroom. Nevertheless, benefits certainly outweigh the drawbacks. Despite safeguards in place to prevent the spread of novel coronavirus, and the school year potentially canceled for thousands of students, Google Classroom is an integrating spot, considering the current state of affairs. Its usage is safe. It takes about half an hour to learn how to use it. Educators can post in an ad-hoc fashion all the essential materials, assignments, and quizzes. The software may assist private tutors, as well as home-school parents.

Chapter 6: How to get the most out of google classroom learning?

Google Classroom streamlines student-work management — announcement, assignment, selection, grading, reviews, and return. It has saved a lot of work hours for teachers. The digital job of grading can be tedious without a reliable workflow and a particular strategy. Google Classroom makes it more useful to collaborate with students — but only if you are aware of how Classroom works and how to use it to your advantage. With a few tips and strategies, Google Classroom can be even more successful in making it productive and effective.

Hack # 1: Better organized work

Use the organizational structure that is feasible for you. If your classwork page was a folder-stuffed filing cabinet, what would you place on those tabs? There are a host of systems that you can use. And thankfully, you'll be able to change your mind. Themes are too easy to modify. Themes to rename, add and remove are so simple. You can turn to a whole new organizational system in a matter of minutes if one does not fit for you.

Here are some examples you could use of the structures:

a. Classify by week

b. Classify by Unit

c. Filter by subject

d. Order by file form

Of course, you can change all of these. But having some suggestions can help you figure out which one suits you best — or at least which one you would like to try first.

Organize each subtopic more thoroughly. For example, the organizational structure can smoothly go deep into two levels—chapters and lessons. Decide how you are going to type it into the topics, and it suits perfectly. Then, stick to it. You just get a chapter and a lesson here merely by typing them in the name. Consistency keeps things perfect! It will make it much easier for students to search for the topics. They can be quicker to find what they need. With multiple levels of the organization, you don't need an official function in Google Classroom. Just create one for yourself!

Using emoji and parenthetical abbreviations as tags might be helpful. Assume you have various characteristics of your items on the Google Classroom page, for instance:

- Some might have images.
- Many of those things could be published
- Some could derive from different academic subjects
- Some might have different types (poetry versus short story versus novel)

- Others might just be interesting or funny stuff you want to share with students.

Assign an emoji in the name for any of those characteristics. Indeed, you already have an emoji keyboard on mobile devices! (If not, look at how you can connect one to your keyboard.) Use an extension like Emoji Keyboard on Chromebooks and computers running the Google Chrome web browser.

To build emoji, use the Ctrl + Cmd + Spacebar keyboard shortcut on Macs.

If your assignment involves a photo, is a written assignment and is a social studies activity, you could use one emoji for each. To use this, think about what attributes students may be looking for in your classwork. Using an emoji lets them, in a glance, locate their task. Don't like using emoji? (Or, would you like to add a second layer of tagging?) Alternatively, try the text tags. For instance, any research project-related activity could be tagged with the abbreviation (RES).

Now, you are fully ready to take charge of a well-organized Google class.

Find a framework for the organization.

Fill in subtopics.

To add tags to classwork, using emoji or text abbreviations.

Either use one such strategy, choose two, or all three! Then watch your Google Classroom fall in line with your hopes and dreams of organizing!

Hack # 2: Reminder about the older material

To put relevant older content back to the attention of the students, use moving to the top. This simple act bumps the top of the class stream with an assignment, announcement, or question. Use this if students have not turned up a task or if you want to remind them of a deadline to come.

Hack # 3: Using the "Student" tab to email everyone simultaneously

In the "Students" tab, email each student in a class. When you click the "Students" tab, click the checkbox to highlight each student. Click "Actions" and "Email." It is nice to call special attention to what you want to communicate to students or to communicate in a longer form.

Hack # 4: Using the relevant comment type

There are various kinds of comments you can leave in the Classroom for students. Understanding how each one works will increase productivity and effectiveness.

- **Making class comments:** Insert a statement "outside" an assignment or notification into your class stream. This will make the statement available to the entire class (vital if it's an answer to a problem that everybody may have).

- **Making private comments:** Do so by viewing student results and clicking on a student individually. The comment bar at the bottom on the right, where you can see student submissions, adds a message that only the student can see (important if it has sensitive grade information or feedback).

- **Comments to be added in a doc/slide/sheet/drawing:** Do this by clicking on the student file that he/she submitted. After highlighting what you wish to comment on, press the black speech bubble button. It makes a very pointed emphasis on particular things in student work (important for input to be very exact).

Hack # 5: Sharing "right now" links using announcements

Announcements place content in the classroom stream without the need for students to hand in an assignment. Use them to provide important links, docs/files, and videos for students, which they will need right away. (If this is a resource which they would frequently use, add the resource to the "About" tab instead.)

Hack # 6: Using the keyboard, rather than the mouse

Using the keyboard commands, do away with the clicks of the mouse every time. Google Classroom's best one: When entering classes, type the grade for the assignment of a specific student, then press the down key to hit the next student. Loop with keystrokes in place of mouse clicks for students to save lots of time.

Hack # 7: Posts' reuse

Do not recreate assignments, announcements, or questions similar to those that you have already created. Press the "+" option in the bottom right-hand corner and select "reuse message." Choose your previously generated task, announcement, or request. You should update and change it before reposting it. You can also opt to make new copies of all the attachments you used before when you revisit a message.

Hack # 8: All grades in one location

In the top left of the Classroom, click the three lines button, and select "Work" at the top. Here you can find all the tasks in one place for all of your classes. Scroll down the list and get at one spot on top of everything.

Hack # 9: Get Classroom emails the way you want them

Do you spend too much time removing Classroom email messages, and wishing you could turn them off? At the top left of the Classroom, press the three lines button, and select "Settings" at the bottom. The checkbox allows you to turn off email notifications. (Or if you turn it off and wish you could get emails, that's where you turn it on!)

Hack # 10: Get others' ideas and opinions

Educators who use Google Classroom also hang out in other online forums where you could read their posts and ask questions. Here are a few suggestions:

- Google Classroom Group on Google Plus
- Mobile Applications for Education Group on Google Plus (with a Google Classroom category)
- Twitter hashtag: # Google Classroom (for Google Classroom-specific posts)
- Twitter hashtag: # Google EDU (for general Google Classroom updates)
- General Pinterest tools on Google Classroom
- A Pinterest board by Shake Up Learning

Hack # 11: Get the features Classroom needs through feedbacks

Have a suggestion for a new feature in Google Classroom? You can do something, but wish you could do something more manageable? That type of input is what Google Classroom wants from the teachers. Click on the "?" at the bottom left of the screen and pick 'Send Feedback.' According to a member of the Google Classroom team, somebody in their group reads every single feedback item sent their way. That is how they have made all of the significant improvements to the Google Classroom app. And the more frequent a request for a feature, the more likely it will be put into effect. So give reviews, and always give them!

Hack # 12: By posting a question, let the students support each other

Teachers needn't answer every question! They should provide the students with the power to help each other. To create a question for a specific task or mission, use the "+" icon. This can act as a platform of discussion, where students can support one another. (Of course, you should also look at the topic to make sure it's correct and timely.)

Hack # 13: Add learning targets

That is not as much a convenience case as it is great pedagogy. It will always remind you about the unit plan or the regular curricular, keeping you grounded.

The inclusion of the learning targets in each assignment or activity would keep reminding the students what the aim of each learning activity is.

Conclusion

Most analysts believe that online learning is taking over as the future of education. Online education shows an upward trend, especially in the prevailing year 2020. A distance learning program may be either a full distance learning or a combination of distance learning and conventional (called hybrid or blended) classroom instruction. Google Classroom is productively integrated with other Google resources like Calendar, Google Docs, Photos, Drive, and more. Educators would be able to build classes, set assignments, send feedback to the individuals, and see all features in one place. Video assignments encourage collaboration and make interactions more comfortable. Google Classroom lets students work together in several ways. Teachers may facilitate online conversations between students and teachers and assign group projects inside the Classroom. Students may collaborate, completing tasks as assigned to them. Students can also collaborate on Google Docs and can quickly share their work with teachers. Through this platform, by centralizing e-learning materials in one cloud-based location, users can go paperless and stop worrying about printing, storing, or even losing the learners' tasks. Unless you already own a personal Google Password, it can be challenging to handle Google Accounts.

Google Classroom does not allow access to multi-domain. Event feed doesn't change automatically, so learners need to review and refresh to avoid missing essential announcements periodically. Thus, Google Classroom comes with both benefits and drawbacks.

Nevertheless, the benefits far outweigh the cons. Instructors may fill in subtopics and apply tags to classwork, using emoji or text abbreviations, to find a suitable structure for a well-organized Google class. Reviews and feedbacks are critical for bringing in new functionality to the Classroom at Google platform. Teachers can use announcements to provide the students with essential links, docs/files, and videos they'll need immediately. Teachers don't need to answer every question! They should give the students the power of mutual support. Use the icon "+" to construct a query for a given task or project. It will serve as a discussion forum where students will encourage each other. Having the learning goals attached to each task or activity in Google's Classroom will keep reminding the students what each learning activity aims to be. With a few tips and strategies, Google Classroom could be made productive, efficient, and even more useful.

References

Distance education. (2020). Retrieved 2020, from **https://en.wikipedia.org/wiki/Distance_education**

Kang, T. (2020). South Korea's Coronavirus-Era Online Learning Hits Snag. Retrieved 2020, from **https://thediplomat.com/2020/04/south-koreas-coronavirus-era-online-learning-hits-snag/**

Types of Online Courses | CAS Online Education. (2020). Retrieved 2020, from **https://oe.uoregon.edu/types-of-online-courses-2/**

Classroom API overview - Classroom Help. (2020). Retrieved 2020, from **https://support.google.com/edu/classroom/answer/6253304?hl=en&ref_topic=7175285**

Google Classroom Reviews: Pricing & Software Features 2020 - Financesonline.com. (2020). Retrieved 2020, from **https://reviews.financesonline.com/p/google-classroom/**

The beginners' guide to Google Classroom. (2020). Retrieved 2020, from **https://www.bookwidgets.com/blog/2017/05/the-beginners-guide-to-google-classroom**

A Timeline of Google Classroom's March to Replace Learning Management Systems - EdSurge News. (2020). Retrieved 2020, from **https://www.edsurge.com/news/2016-09-27-a-timeline-of-google-classroom-s-march-to-replace-learning-management-systems**

8 Myths About Online Learning: The Truth Behind the Screen. (2020). Retrieved 2020, from **https://www.rasmussen.edu/student-experience/college-life/myths-about-online-learning/**

Era, 1. (2020). 15 minutes of Fame: Online Learning in the Coronavirus Era. Retrieved 2020, from **https://www.al-fanarmedia.org/2020/04/15-minutes-of-fame-online-learning-in-the-coronavirus-era/**